W9-ACC-540

THE GERMAN LIBRARY

Wilhelm Busch
and others

GERMAN
SATIRICAL
WRITINGS

EDITED BY DIETER P. LOTZE AND VOLKMAR SANDER
FOREWORD BY JOHN SIMON

German Satirical Writings

The German Library : Volume 50

Volkmar Sander, General Editor

Wilhelm Busch and Others

GERMAN SATIRICAL WRITINGS

Edited by Dieter P. Lotze
and Volkmar Sander

Foreword by John Simon

CONTINUUM · NEW YORK

1984

The Continuum Publishing Company
370 Lexington Avenue, New York, NY 10017

Copyright © 1984 by The Continuum Publishing Company

Foreword © 1984 by John Simon
Introduction © 1984 by Dieter P. Lotze

Printed in the United States of America

Library of Congress Cataloging in Publication Data

Main entry under title:

German satirical writings.

(The German library; v. 50)
Includes index.
1. Satire, German—Translations into English.
2. German literature—19th century—Translations into
English. 3. German literature—20th century—Translations
into English. 4. Satire, English—Translations from
German. 5. English literature—Translations from German.
I. Busch, Wilhelm, 1832–1908. II. Lotze, Dieter P.
III. Sander, Volkmar. IV. Series.
PT1113.G47 1984   837'.008   83-26158
ISBN 0-8264-0284-4
ISBN 0-8264-0285-2 (pbk.)

Acknowledgments will be found on page 319,
which constitutes an extension of the copyright page.

Contents

Foreword

"Difficile est saturam non scribere," wrote Juvenal. "Satire," observed George S. Kaufman, "is what closes on Saturday night." Between these two remarks, some nineteen centuries apart, can be inscribed the parabola of satire. The first-and-second-century Roman poet, recording the follies and vices of his world, found nothing more appropriate than castigation through satire. The twentieth-century American playwright, noting the public's non-support of satirical plays, coined a piece of fake, funny etymology to serve as epitaph. To be sure, like most generalizations, mine, too, oversimplifies. There were poets in Rome who did as other Romans did, and wrote no satires. And to this day an occasional satirical work fares well, even on the stage. But not, perhaps, in America.

Yet what is satire really? Like so many terms whose meanings are taken for granted, it has never been conclusively defined. Or, rather, it has been defined in many, contradictory ways. There is Swift's famous assertion about his output: "Yet malice never was his aim;/ He lashed the vice but spared the name./ No individual could resent,/ Where thousands equally were meant./ His satire points out no defect/ But what all mortals may correct;/ For he abhorr'd that senseless tribe/ Who call it humor when they gibe." Against this humane view of satire (to which, by the way, Swift did not strictly adhere), there is the tradition that the earliest satirists, the Greek poets Archilochus and Hipponax (seventh and sixth century B.C., respectively), caused their victims to hang themselves. The distinguished modern scholar, Wolfgang Kayser, characterizes satire in *Das sprachliche Kunstwerk (The Verbal Art Work)* as having "a deliberate hostile tendency aiming at fundamental abolition." Although he does not state whether this hostility is directed at specific, named or at least identifiable, individuals, or whether it attacks defects *in abstracto,* such an inimical stance can easily make people feel uncomfortable. And though, again in Swift's words, satire is "a sort of glass, wherein beholders do generally discover everybody's face but their own," somewhere in the gut there may occur a twinge of unpleasant recognition.

Let us recall, too, that the first major satirist, Aristophanes, did not spare the individual, and savaged with equal comic harshness those, like Cleon, who deserved it, and those, like Socrates, Aeschylus, and Euripides, who didn't. It is all very well for the master of French verse satire, Boileau, to say (as translated by the English master, Dryden) that "satire, ever moral, ever new,/ Delights the reader and instructs him, too./ She, if good sense refine her sterling page,/ Oft shakes some rooted folly of the age," but some satires, and often not the worst, thrive on excess unrefined by good sense. Another famous definition, by Lady Mary Wortley Montagu (1689–1762), "Satire should like a polished razor keen,/ Wound with a touch that's scarcely felt or seen," raises a troubling question: Is not, though its slicing off may not be felt, the missing limb or lopped-off head a fairly serious problem for its former owner?

The difficulty is partly semantic. Some literary terms, such as panegyric or elegy, pretty much define themselves. Not so satire, which seems to come from the Latin *satura* (short for *satura lanx*), later *satira,* which meant, as Eric Partridge puts it in *Origins,* "a macédoine of fruits or vegetables or a composite dish of meats, hence a mixed literary composition." The mixture was originally a thematic or formal olla podrida, as in Ennius (239–169 B.C.), whose poetry had nothing of the modern satire about it, and Lucilius (180–102 B.C.), whose verse had it to a modest degree. Satire in roughly its modern form stems from two later Latin progenitors, Horace and Juvenal, whose own models were the Greeks, Menippus and Bion, respectively. To quote J. A. Cuddon's *A Dictionary of Literary Terms,* "Horace is the tolerant, urbane and amused spectator of the human scene; Juvenal is bitter, misanthropic and consumed with indignation." We could say that the difference is as between irony and sarcasm or insinuation and invective, except that one man perceives as irony what the other sees as sarcasm. For example, when Heine in the frequently satirical *Die romantische Schule (The Romantic School)* claims for the protagonist of Fouqué's *Sigurd the Dragonslayer* "as much courage as a hundred lions and as much intelligence as two asses," is that irony or sarcasm? Leaving Fouqué's feelings aside, would the average reader experience this as a funny and legitimate barb or as cruel and unusually sardonic punishment?

To confuse the issue even further, the same author may be alternately Horatian and Juvenalian; thus the satire in Büchner's *Leonce und Lena* would be the former; in *Woyzeck,* the latter. Even within a single work the satiric point of view may shift, consciously or unconsciously. Take the first piece in this book, *Max and Moritz.* Is Busch's satire directed against the two nasty little pranksters? If so, they make an awfully easy target; moreover, Busch seems to enjoy their mischief so much as to sound almost more conspiratorial than condemnatory. Certainly the good burghers who are being victimized look and sound silly and conventional to the point of almost deserving the tricks played on them. And, however rotten, the boys do not merit being ground to a horrible death, no matter how comically worded and illustrated. Or do they, perpetrating criminal juvenilia that promise full-fledged adult delinquecies, merit it after all? The answers are not easily come by, but, whatever the case, there is more to *Max and Moritz* than a simple cautionary tale served up to simpleminded children by their simplistic parents.

And what then of *Balduin Bählamm,* Englished as *Clement Dove?* This mock epic seems to be pillorying a benighted poetaster, a white-collar worker with artistic pretensions. But, surely, the villagers who torment him for footling missteps with ludicrous but painful punishments are no decent, forbearing Christians. Again, on whose side is Busch? Is he with ostensible common sense against the quixotic, or is he giving us a veiled parable about the artist's victimization by society—for even a toothache becomes a major calamity only when the supposed dentist proves a quack. Or is satire a double-edged sword that cuts in both directions, a common phenomenon in Brecht, in whose plays often nobody's point of view is fully condonable.

To return to the attempts at definition, however. Humbert Wolfe, a minor but charming British poet, essayist, and satirist, begins his *Notes on English Verse Satire* (1929) as follows:

> The satirist holds a place halfway between the preacher and the wit. He has the purpose of the first and uses the weapons of the second. He must both hate and love. For what impels him to write is not less the hatred of wrong and injustice than a love of the right and just. So much he shares with the prophet. But he seeks to affect the minds of men, not by the congruities of virtue, but by the incongruities of vice, and in that he partakes of the wit. For as laughter dispels care by showing that as one thing is, so all may be, absurd, so it attacks wickedness by robbing it of its pretensions.

Blessed, uncomplicated definition of 1929! By 1957, Northrop Frye, in his *Anatomy of Criticism* makes matters much more elaborate by postulating three phases of satire. Summarizing, we can describe the first, which Frye calls low-norm satire, as one in which societal conventions are upheld by a cunning, self-depreciating realist (or, in the Greek term, *eiron*), who outwits or overthrows the powerful, self-exalting overreacher (or *alazon*), and the norm ends up upheld. Second-phase or *"ingénu"* satire has an outsider (the Voltairean *ingénu*) questioning the establishment's values, and finding them deficient or defective from his own pragmatic, honest standpoint. Finally, third-phase or high-norm satire turns against everything—even common sense, which has its own dogmas (chiefly that sense experience is reliable), and satire itself to the extent that it is based on common sense. So we get a satire of delirium, which Frye illustrates with aspects of Rabelais and Joyce, notably the frenzied word catalogues. This is what we get in most of Morgenstern's *Galgenlieder (Gallows Songs)*, in which logic is, delicately or enthusiastically, stood on its head and made to dance on it.

The diversity of satire is done ample justice to in this compilation, even if it draws on the work of only four writers. In fact, a great many fruitful speculations about satire are possible just by comparing and contrasting the philosophies and techniques of Wilhelm Busch, Christian Morgenstern, Kurt Tucholsky, and Erich Kästner. And also by comparing their lives. In *Satire: A Critical Anthology*, the editors, John Russell and Ashley Brown, summarize a widely-held notion: "The overturning of stock beliefs held by majorities seems to accord with the phenomenon that satirists frequently have emerged from mean conditions, even slavery, and also from backgrounds of nobility. They have thus been able to scrutinize conventions from below and from above. Satire is hardly a middle-class art." This makes good sense and fits in with Frye's second category, *ingénu* satire. But then we read in Frye himself that "to attack anything, writer and audience must agree on its undesirability." These propositions would seem contradictory if it weren't for the self-contradictions of human nature. Thus Busch was the son of a grocer and Kästner of a washerwoman; Tucholsky was a Jew, which made him first figuratively, then, in his Nazi-induced exile, literally an outsider; Morgenstern was set apart from the bourgeois mentality by his descent from landscape painters on both sides of his family, and from bourgeois robustiousness by a fatal lung disease that carried him off at forty-two.

Outsiders by origin and originality of vision, these four nevertheless hit upon ways of garnering public endorsement. In the case of Busch, it was simple misunderstanding: the public enjoyed his pretty or witty pictures and the seeming innocence of the verse that resembled familiar doggerel *(Knittelvers)* but actually played subtly ominous games with it; they looked into his work as into a mere funhouse mirror, though it was in fact a monument to their outer and inner ugliness. Morgenstern had a mystical streak even in his grotesqueries and nonsense poems that finally led him to Rudolf Steiner and anthroposophy, and to the writing of undistinguished mystical effusions. Still, the combination of otherworldliness and satirical whimsy makes *The Gallows Songs* look less like a slap at and denial of bourgeois realities than like tomfooleries for bright children or diversions for the Nietzschean child in man.

Tucholsky was, plainly and seemingly simply, so damned funny, and so feuilletonistically able to sensationalize or oversimplify, as to seduce the *Spiessbürger* probably on the Swiftian principle of discovering in his glass everybody's face except their own. As for Kästner, he was the principal exponent of *die neue Sachlichkeit* (the new objectivity, or reality, or detachment—the German word has all those meanings), a movement that rejuvenated verse by looking reality more brazenly in the eye, and more anatomically in the gut. Here, then, were social, sexual, and political situations viewed not always satirically or even humorously, but in so observant, penetrating, detached a way that the old actions, utterances, conditions assumed a disorienting—sometimes hilarious, sometimes stabbing—newness, constituting a sort of satire by implication. For behind the specifics there was that unnamed but implicit butt, Modern Life, that is, an economy, politics, and morality that allowed these ludicrous or pitiful things to be. Both the humor and the pity had an edge of absurdity provided by the dispassionateness of the observation and the irreverence of the imagery, by the pungent immediacy of the diction and the cool regularity (but not monotony) of meter, rhyme, and stanza form.

It is both revealing and challenging to examine how similar themes and motifs are handled by our four authors. Take, for example, a German poet in a Paris park, whether it is Tucholsky in "Parc Monceau" or Kästner in "Jardin du Luxembourg" (not included here, but easily available to anyone with some knowledge of German). These parks lie very close to paradise, as Kästner says of his, but either the pastoral idyll itself (in Kästner) is fraught with intimations of life's responsibilities and uncertainties or (in Tucholsky) the *rus in urbe* is surrounded by lowering political realities that obtrude in the wonderfully ironic last line, *"und ruh von meinem Vaterlande aus"* (and [I] rest up from my fatherland). Either way, there is a fragility and absurdity in human bliss: the child in Tucholsky's park serenely picking its nose; the tumult and jubilation in Kästner's, wafting by like music, but only shouting, after all. The satire is less in what is described than in what can be deduced: the crudeness of our pleasures, the impermanence built into our joy.

Or compare Busch's Clement Dove, when, in chapter 5, he escapes from the earwig only to catch the songbird's droppings, with the poem "Philanthropisch" by Morgenstern (again not included here, but available easily enough both in German and English). Much the same disenchantment with bucolic Edens prevails in both, and both depend for their effects on ingenious prosody and verbal and syntactical pyrotechnics. But Busch is discursive where Morgenstern is terse, and Busch's would-be poetic ninny is less ecumenical than Morgenstern's "nervous man in a meadow." But if Morgenstern's three quatrains work through their awesome lapidariness, Busch's leisurely expansiveness scores through spectacular pratfalls.

Finally, a three-way comparison on the theme of the passing of love. In Busch's lyric, "Die Liebe war nicht geringe" ("The love affair was not negligible"), the satiric effect is in the contrast between the romantic excesses and arduously cleared hurdles of the first two stanzas and the dismalness of the third, where the wife sits knitting or darning socks while the husband reads to her charily such passages from the morning paper as he deems fit for her consumption—nothing like the "thousand things" they formerly exchanged. The triumph of quotidian drabness is further developed in Tucholsky's prose sketch, "Mr. Wendriner Gives a Dinner Party," a monologue in which the husband gripes about the just finished party and a lot of other things while his conjugal partner, trying slavishly to please him, cleans up and suffers in silence as he basks in complaint. In "Sachliche Romanze," Kästner scrutinizes a couple who, after eight years of unmarried togetherness, have fallen out of love. The emphasis is on the couple's incomprehension of what went wrong. The poem is fundamentally sad, which, though etymologically related to "sated," which in turn is related to "satire," is not the right mood for that genre. What does, however, make it satirical, albeit gently, is the befuddled helplessness of these lovers who cannot hold on to their love or even grasp the cause of its demise. Busch's satire is ironically pessimistic, Tucholsky's rambunctiously grotesque yet also realistic, Kästner's muted with misery.

Let me quote Humbert Wolfe once more: "A thing may be ridiculous and yet not laughable. It may affront reason without surprising it, as it may be in the last degree witty without being funny." Satire, as the following modest anthology of nevertheless considerable scope demonstrates, can come to grips with all these curious emotional hybrids, this macédoine of feelings and olla podrida of actions, just as it can with major vices, and make us either laugh out loud or wryly smile, and try to do better. Or, failing that, at least to understand.

And by showing us how satire, still quite recognizable in Busch, becomes progressively alienated from itself—in the comic monody of Tucholsky's "Ideal and Reality," in the choric lament of Kästner's "Typist Chorus," in the metrical hieroglyph of Morgenstern's "Fish's Night Song"—the book confirms Kaufman's epigram about the lean times on which satire has fallen. It does, after all, depend on the complicity of the author with an enlightened minority; but in a world in which the crowd, democratically or otherwise, swallows up the individual, satire is deprived of both its producers and its consumers. The genre is having a hard time of it. May this book help reverse the trend!

JOHN SIMON

Introduction

In 1919, Kurt Tucholsky, writing for the liberal journal *Die Weltbühne*, reviewed *Der Gingganz (The Wentall)*, the posthumous collection of Christian Morgenstern's whimsical poetry. The essay emphasized an important parallel:

> Morgenstern is the Busch of our days. Just as our fathers used to have fun with the Low German woodcut drawings of that great philosopher—between you and me: in that respect I am my own dad—now a whole new generation is roaring with laughter over Palmström, Korf, and Aunt Kunkel. It is really delightful: you double up with laughter, later on, having become more serious, you admire his profound poetry which only at the very last moment is turned into something comical—and finally you realize that you have learned a philosophical principle.

When, on the occasion of his seventieth birthday in 1969, Erich Kästner was made an honorary member of the Wilhelm Busch Society, he gratefully accepted and said: "After all, Wilhelm Busch is one of my spiritual grandfathers. (The other one is Heinrich Heine.)"

A volume on German satire could, of course, concentrate on various literary epochs and on the characteristic works they brought forth, from medieval animal epics and Walther von der Vogelweide's attacks on the political power of the papacy, through the bitter religious debates of the Reformation period, to the eighteenth century and the Age of Enlightenment with Lessing's crusades and Lichtenberg's biting aphorisms, the spirited satires of the young rebels of the Storm and Stress movement, or the aggressive

Xenia of Goethe and Schiller. German Romanticism and the post-Napoleonic era of *Junges Deutschland,* culminating in Heine's writings, could furnish a wealth of material. Yet, given the space limitations of a collection like ours, the focus on the Age of Bismarck and the troubled times in its wake seemed particularly appropriate. This period has certainly left its indelible mark on our century. As Erich Kästner pointed out very succinctly in his poem "The Ascent of Man," humanity has made giant progress in its technological development without experiencing any moral growth, and many of Wilhelm Busch's critical observations of the 1870s or 1880s appear hardly dated at all to the modern reader. In addition, his enormous impact on his times and the seminal role he played for the work of later writers and artists cannot be overestimated, a view stressed by the two outstanding twentieth-century satirists quoted above.

Busch (1832–1908) was born in a North German village, the oldest of the seven children of the local grocer who wanted his son to become an engineer. Busch, however, decided to study art, but soon was increasingly unsure about his artistic ability and his goals. In 1858, his talent as a cartoonist was discovered by the publisher of the humorous and satirical journal *Fliegende Blätter,* who invited him to become a regular contributor. Busch's career as a painter had ended, that of the creator of humorous drawings and—a little later—funny poetic captions had been launched. Single drawings and illustrations for the texts of others soon gave way to the unique blend of graphic art and whimsical verse that was to amuse millions and that made him the most popular and most widely quoted German author.

It is generally acknowledged today that much of Busch's popularity was based on a misconception, encouraged, however, by the artist himself. The first of his great "picture stories," *Max und Moritz* of 1865, was an immediate success and has remained one of the world's most popular children's books. Busch's contemporaries, and subsequent generations of parents, saw his "little children's epic" as a moralistic and pedagogically effective tale. This narrative of juvenile crime and its punishment in a rural setting appeared to teach a simple lesson, just as Heinrich Hoffmann's immensely popular *Struwwelpeter* of 1848 had done: Bad boys will have to pay dearly for their misdeeds.

It took the twentieth century with its experience of dramatic societal changes and its questioning of traditional values to recognize the satire beneath what had been considered mainly entertaining humor. Busch unmasks and ridicules the world of the middle-class establishment. Widow Bolte hides her essentially materialistic attitude behind pseudo-Romantic verbiage when she discovers the death of her chickens. Tailor Billy, popular in the community because his skills are needed, overreacts dramatically to the boys' teasing and reveals that his calm composure is an attempt to compensate for his basic insecurity. Master Lampel, the teacher, is what his name implies: *Lämpel,* "little lamp," is indeed a small luminary in the world of scholarship. "To be content" in the enjoyment of creature comforts is the highest human achievement according to his philosophy of life. Kind Uncle Fritz also values such "earthly joys" above everything else. The natural role of younger family members is to contribute to his comfort. When the May beetles interrupt his night's rest, he goes berserk and "stamps and tramples, slaps and hits" until the bedroom floor is covered with insect corpses. To the "pious baker," putting Max and Moritz to death in his oven seems a fitting punishment for their attempted theft of some pretzels. Farmer Klein, in cheerful complicity with the miller, finally executes the bad boys, who had caused him to lose some grain, by having them ground to pieces. All members of the community rejoice in the knowledge that the troublemakers who had disturbed their peace and quiet and threatened their value system are gone forever:

> That entire place, in short,
> Buzzed with joy at the report;
> And they offered heartfelt thanks
> For deliverance from pranks.

It is ironic indeed that this satirical look at the *petit bourgeois* of rural Germany not only endeared Busch to the very class he was caricaturizing but also established him as the grandfather—or godfather—of an art form usually considered typically American. In 1897, *Max und Moritz* became the model for Rudolph Dirks' *Katzenjammer Kids,* whose very title, and mock-Teutonic accent point to its German roots. Thus Busch's "picture story" became the immediate forerunner of today's comic strip. Yet Dirks, too, saw only the slapstick humor of the boys' pranks, and neither his strip nor most of its direct successors imitated Busch's satirical stance.

Busch's "adult" picture stories of the 1870s and 1880s, which delighted an ever-growing audience, poked fun at various human and societal shortcomings. He attacked religious prejudice and hypocrisy in *Der heilige Antonius von Padua (St. Anthony of Padua)* of 1870 and *Die fromme Helene (Pious Helen)* of 1873 and mocked the complacency of the burgher of the *Gründerjahre,* the period of prosperity and economic growth after the German victory over France, in his *Knopp Trilogy: Abenteuer eines Junggesellen (Adventures of a Bachelor)* of 1875, *Herr und Frau Knopp (Mr. and Mrs. Knopp)* of 1876, and *Julchen (Julie)* of 1877. Today's reader and viewer will gain valuable insights into the attitudes and philosophies of the middle class of the Bismarck era by following the adventures of roly-poly Tobias Knopp who seeks a wife in order to make sure that his eventual demise will have an impact on somebody, who settles down to the same self-satisfied enjoyment of creature comforts as some of the burghers in *Max und Moritz,* who finally sires a daughter and then considers his mission in life fulfilled after having successfully married her off.

One of the secrets behind the continuing success of these and other tales may be Busch's ability to present a satiric caricature that is at the same time sympathetic and allows the audience to identify with some of the characters portrayed. Busch's favorite topic remained the tragicomedy of everyday human life. Even his two long animal tales, *Fipps der Affe (Fips the Monkey)* of 1879 and *Plisch und Plum (Plish and Plash)* of 1882, the adventures of two mischievous dogs and their young masters, attack mainly human failings: greed and envy, vanity and intellectual pretentiousness, stupidity and cruelty, hypocrisy and shallowness. In both *Balduin Bählamm, der verhinderte Dichter (Clement Dove, the Poet Thwarted)* of 1883 and *Maler Klecksel (Painter Squirtle)* of 1884, Busch juxtaposed the world of the bourgeois and that of the artist. But the fact that in these picture stories the artist's position, too, is viewed from the vantage point of the middle class makes them appear like burlesque variations on the theme which Thomas Mann was to treat twenty years later in *Tonio Kröger:* the burgher gone astray in the world of art. Clement Dove tries to use poetry as an escape from the drabness of everyday life. His ultimate failure is due to the hostility of his surroundings as well as to his own inadequacy and his misconception of the purpose and meaning of art. Squirtle, on the other hand, embarks on a career as a painter—just as his creator had done—only to end as the happy and self-satisfied owner of the "White Horse Tavern."

A comparison of the drawings for the three pictorial narratives in this volume demonstrates not only Busch's development and growing maturity as a cartoonist, but also the extent to which modern technology aided him in communicating his artistry: *Adventures of a Bachelor* was the last of his works for which the drawings had to be cut in wood for printing. The pictures for his later books, including *Clement Dove,* could be reproduced photomechanically, thus allowing him far greater freedom of artistic expression.

Busch's poetry, frequently attacking the same targets as his picture stories, has met with much less popular success. Without the funny drawings, it was harder for his readers to overlook the satirical intent. Also, his contemporaries expected a poem to be "poetic" in language and content. The skillful incorporation of colloquialisms into his verse, his puns and deliberate distortions of words for the sake of a humorous rhyme, widely applauded in his picture stories, were considered inappropriate for poetic expression. It did not help with the reading public of the Age of Bismarck—or, for that matter, with later audiences—that some of these techniques, as well as his tendency to create a certain mood and then surprise the reader by destroying or ridiculing it, had been pioneered by Heinrich Heine.

Tucholsky's description of Morgenstern's poetry applies to much of Busch's verse as well. "Philosophical principles" frequently hide beneath the comic surface, and a careful examination reveals not only his criticism of society and of human foibles, but also the impact of Schopenhauer on the author and his attempt to overcome that influence. The bird who decides to sing in the face of certain death represents a positive realism that is also part of Busch's world view, although this poem should not be seen as his ultimate definition of humor. Busch's unsentimental view of the human animal is as pertinent today as it was in his days.

At first glance, the world of Christian Morgenstern (1871–1914) appears vastly different. Instead of caricature, of satiric distortion of the real world, we witness here the creation of a new universe out of familiar linguistic fragments. This mysterious but somehow quite plausible environment is populated by creatures like the Moon Sheep, the Hawken Chick, the Nosobame (which, contrary to the poet's expectations, has in the meantime found its permanent place in German encyclopedias), the Twelve Nix, or the Wentall whose origin and existence should not puzzle us any more than those of the lonely knee that continues to live and to march. What Morgenstern accomplished through his play with language, one of his contemporaries was soon to attempt in visual form. The drawings and paintings of Paul Klee (1879–1940) present a striking parallel to the world of the *Gallows Songs,* and it is not surprising that some of his works were inspired by Morgenstern poems.

When the *Gallows Songs* were published in 1905, Morgenstern, the son and grandson of landscape painters and himself originally destined for that career, had already established a certain reputation as a lyrical neo-Romantic poet. Little wonder that many critics were baffled by what one reviewer called "a symptom of the brain fatigue of our age." Eventually, Morgenstern, in the guise of "Dr. Jeremias Mueller," offered explanatory notes for several of the poems. These comments make his satiric intentions even more obvious. Line-by-line annotations for "The Twelve Nix" poke fun at the pedantic scholarly approach that loses track of the main issue. In a similar vein, "Mueller" speculates about the geographic location of the offensive "Picket Fence." The possible political prophecy of "Ding Dong Dang" as referring to events of the year 1908 is discussed with mock seriousness. Finally, "Fish's Night Song," which had quite logically reduced the poetry of the mute creature to mere metric scheme, is wittily called the "most profound German poem."

To the superficial reader, *Palmström* of 1910 seemed somewhat different and easier to accept. Palmstroem and his friend Korf were seen as two real—albeit eccentric—human beings. Everybody had encountered the type of jokes "invented" by Korf, and the absurd logic of the "Impossible Fact" was altogether convincing, even to those who were not students of German idealistic philosophy but naive believers in a system of law and order. Yet, the difference between the world of the *Gallows Songs* and that of *Palmström* is only on the surface. Both call into question commonly accepted views of what exists or of what can exist. In doing so, in tackling the problem of appearance and reality, Morgenstern's whimsical verse is not too distant from some of Busch's satire. As several critics have noticed, Morgenstern is also indebted to Wilhelm Busch in his approach to meter and language.

Palma Kunkel appeared posthumously in 1916 as war was raging in Europe. *Der Gingganz (The Wentall)* came out in 1919 as mankind was reviewing the destruction it had wrought. By that time, Morgenstern's satiric stance of calling into question the rationality and sanity of the world was no longer revolutionary. Dadaism was in part employing his techniques for similar ends, and Surrealism, recognizing with Sigmund Freud and with Morgenstern that dreams could be as valid as any conscious experience, was reinterpreting the world. Yet, most of the artistic endeavors of the period were lacking the comic element that evokes laughter and leads, in the thoughtful reader of Busch as well as of Morgenstern, to more serious contemplation.

Busch's satire could easily be misread: he himself identified with the class he caricaturized, and the resulting ambiguity is characteristic of most of his work. Similarly, Morgenstern could be dismissed as merely the author of amusing nonsense poetry. But Kurt Tucholsky (1890–1935) and Erich Kästner (1899–1974) left no doubt as to the aims of their attacks. In the spirit of Heinrich Heine, German satire was becoming once again clearly focused and topical, and some of the targets had hardly changed over almost a century. For Tucholsky as well as for Kästner, the experience of the First World War presented an incentive to apply artistic talent to the task of creating a better world. Both fought for social justice and democracy. Both saw as their deadly enemies the traditions and attitudes that had led to senseless bloodshed and destruction and that were now threatening the very life of the young Weimar Republic.

Kurt Tucholsky, the son of a well-to-do Jewish businessman in Berlin, published his first short prose piece in the satirical magazine *Ulk* when he was only seventeen. It was entitled "Fairy Tale" and mocked the ignorance and prejudice of Kaiser Wilhelm II in matters of contemporary art. In several ways, this brief text was indicative of the future direction of Tucholsky's work. As a satirist, he was to ridicule ignorance and arrogance and to attack those in political power. As an observer of the cultural scene, he was to retain a life-long interest in all manifestations of artistic expression and to become an outstanding critic of literature and of the stage. At the same time, the writer who selected the medium of a fairy tale for his attack had a tendency toward the idyllic and was capable of lyrical expression and sentiment.

Above all, however, Tucholsky demonstrated from the very beginning his mastery of style, his keen ear for linguistic nuances, his ability to select the most effective form for whatever he wanted to communicate. He could be passionate or detached, witty or blunt, subjective in his opinions as the creative writer he had chosen to be and objective in his analysis of facts as the trained lawyer he was. Quite consistently, these diverse aspects of his approach to writing led to the development of several distinctly different personas. His initial publications, including his first book, *Rheinsberg: Ein Bilderbuch für Verliebte (Rheinsberg: A Picture Book for Lovers)* of 1912, appeared under his name, but he soon adopted a number of pseudonyms. In 1913, he started to contribute regularly to the weekly *Die Schaubühne* (renamed *Die Weltbühne* in 1918) whose left-leaning and increasingly pacifist orientation matched his own views. In 1926, after the death of his long-time mentor and friend Siegfried Jacobsohn who had founded the journal in 1905 and been at its helm ever since, Tucholsky was to take over as its editor for ten months. But he felt uncomfortable with that position and gladly relinquished the reins to Carl von Ossietzky (1889–1938), who was to be among the first persons arrested after Hitler had come to power. To the embarrassment of the Nazis, Ossietzky was awarded the 1935 Nobel Peace Prize while still a prisoner in one of their concentration camps, where he was later murdered.

Die Weltbühne gave Tucholsky the opportunity to develop into several different writers, as it were. As "Ignaz Wrobel," he published some of his most aggressive (and least humorous) articles and essays. Militarism, the excesses of a biased justice system, and the threat to democracy from the political right in general were among Wrobel's favorite targets. A little later, "Peter Panter" started writing his more detached essays, dealing with literature, language ("Someday Somebody Should . . ."), or with philosophical and sociological questions ("Angler, Compleat with Piety," "The Creed of the Bourgeoisie"). A few months after Panter's birth, "Theobald Tiger" emerged who would write only poetry. Tiger's poems ranged from the evocation of lyrical moods to clarion calls to political action. Quite a few were later set to music and became popular *chansons* on the cabaret stage of the Weimar Republic or favorites at labor union rallies. In 1918, Kaspar Hauser appeared on the scene. Like his namesake, the famous foundling of the nineteenth century, he seemed to look at the world with a naive desire to learn and experience. He was to record with apparent objectivity the follies and foibles of his times, whether expressed in a fictitious schoolboy's composition ("Essay on Man") or in the interior monologues of Tucholsky's most popular creation, Herr Wendriner. Hauser's essay on "The Social Psychology of Holes" is one of the finest examples of Tucholsky's prose style.

Later, Tucholsky was to write about the need for those pen names and about their significance:

> A small weekly prefers not to have the same name appear four times in the same issue, and so, for fun, these homunculi came into existence. . . . Pseudonyms are like little human beings; it is dangerous to pretend to be somebody else, to adopt names—a name has a life of its own. And what had started as sort of a game ended as cheerful schizophrenia. . . . It was also useful to exist in five different versions—for who in Germany believes that a political writer can have a sense of humor? that a satirist can be serious? that a playful person can be acquainted with the penal code? that an author of city sketches can write funny verse? Humor tends to discredit.

In 1924, Tucholsky went to Paris as a correspondent for *Die Weltbühne* and *Vossische Zeitung*. He was never again to take up permanent residence in Germany. A poem like "Parc Monceau" shows his appreciation of the liberating atmosphere of Paris. Perhaps it is one more indication of his "cheerful schizophrenia" that he wrote in Paris those pieces that—in language and setting—appear most closely connected with Berlin, the musings of "Herr Wendriner." Wendriner, the Jewish businessman who tries hard to adapt, is perhaps the most successful translation of Busch's Tobias Knopp into terms of the middle class of the Weimar Republic. Millions of "Wendriners," and not all of them Jewish, perished in the holocaust unleashed by those about whom Tucholsky had tried to warn his readers. As early as 1923, he had written in a letter: "I am successful, but I am having no impact." When Karl Kraus (1874–1936), through his one-man enterprise *Die Fackel* in many ways Tucholsky's Viennese comrade-in-arms, stated in 1933, "I just cannot think of anything in connection with Hitler," the same Hitler had already stilled the voice of *Die Weltbühne* and that of Kurt Tucholsky. On December 21, 1935, the author committed suicide in Sweden, where he had lived since 1929.

Erich Kästner, just as Tucholsky, could be considered "schizophrenic" in his literary work. The man who waged some of the most biting attacks on militarism, chauvinism, and the self-satisfied attitude of the bourgeoisie, the uninhibited chronicler of the "new morality" of the 1920s in his 1931 novel *Fabian,* was at the same time the author of sensitive and immensely popular children's books. *Emil und die Detektive (Emil and the Detectives),* his "novel for children" of 1928, was translated into many languages and repeatedly adapted for stage and film versions. *Pünktchen und Anton,* written the same year as *Fabian,* or *Das doppelte Lottchen* of 1949 (made into a film in Hollywood as *The Parent Trap*) have also remained children's favorites in many countries.

Perhaps this contradiction is more apparent than real. Kästner's childhood dream had been to become a teacher. His working-class parents had taken boarders into their small Dresden apartment in order to supplement their meager income, and all these young men happened to be teachers, thus possibly serving as immediate models to young Erich. The adult Kästner realized his dream, although not in the sense he had once imagined. After obtaining a teaching certificate and then going on for a doctorate in German language and literature, he chose a career as a writer. Yet he continued to see his mission as that of an educator. He was able to speak to children as an adult who took them and their problems seriously. He attempted to raise the consciousness of his adult readers through his satire, employing wit and humor as weapons, not merely as instruments of entertainment. In 1946, he wrote:

> Satirists cannot be silent because they are schoolmasters. And schoolmastering is a schoolmaster's job. Well, and in the most

hidden corner of their hearts, shy and surviving despite all the world's foolishness, there blooms that silly, nonsensical hope that, after all, people might possibly become a bit, a tiny bit better if they are abused, begged, insulted, and laughed at often enough. Satirists are idealists.

Kästner's reference to Busch and Heine as his spiritual grandfathers appears entirely justified in view of his goals as well as his techniques. Yet he could have pointed to his intellectual kinship with yet another man, like him a native of Saxony and filled with the same desire to change mankind through his writing. In a very real sense, Kästner was a disciple of Gotthold Ephraim Lessing, whose praise he sang in a brief poem. Thus, despite his modern language and contemporary topics, he was a man of the eighteenth century, a believer in the possibility that human beings could be taught to think and thereby become better.

It is not surprising that Kästner would clash with the Nazis whose ideology was the very antithesis of the philosophy of Enlightenment. They had not forgiven him poems like "Know'st Thou the Land . . ." or "The Other Possibility," and, once in power, would prohibit the publication of his works in Germany and eventually also keep him from publishing abroad. Yet, in spite of these attempts to silence his voice, in spite of repeated arrests by the Gestapo, Kästner decided not to leave his native country as so many outstanding writers had done. He even had the courage to attend the public burning of his books in Berlin. And he survived the Third Reich, sustained by that "silly, nonsensical hope" that was blooming in his heart.

In the title of a 1919 essay, Tucholsky, as Ignaz Wrobel, had asked the question, "What May Satire Do?" His answer was that satire was free to do anything. If one tries to assess the success or failure of Germany's outstanding satirists, a slightly different question poses itself: "What can satire accomplish?" Perhaps the answer cannot be as positive. "Humor tends to discredit." Wilhelm Busch is still primarily seen as the great comic entertainer. Christian Morgenstern, who eventually embraced Rudolf Steiner's anthroposophical views, is popular because of his "nonsense rhymes." Kästner's worldwide success is based on his children's books. And Tucholsky himself, his warnings unheeded, his country plunged into barbarism, took poison. And yet, the spirit of Enlightenment lives on, and satirists will keep on trying.

Several poems and prose pieces included in our selection were especially translated for this volume. Few of Kästner's poems are available in English, and the two collections of Tucholsky's works in translation are now out of print. Max Knight's highly acclaimed renditions of Morgenstern and Walter Arndt's recently published versions of Busch's picture stories and poems are still easily accessible but it is hoped that their inclusion in this volume will establish a new context for authors who deserve to be known better in the English-speaking world.

D. P. L.

WILHELM BUSCH

Max and Moritz

Preface

Ah, the wickedness one sees
Or is told of such as these,
Namely Max and Moritz; there!
Look at the disgraceful pair!

Who, so far from gladly reaching
For the boons of moral teaching,
Chose those very rules to flout
And in secret laugh about.—
But designs of malefaction
Find them keen on instant action!
Teasing folk, tormenting beasts,
Stealing fruit for lawless feasts
Are more fun, as one can tell,
And less troublesome as well,
Than to sit through class or sermon,
Never fidgeting or squirming.—
Looking at the sequel, though:
Woe, I say, and double woe!!—
How it all at last came out
Chills the heart to think about.
That's why all the tricks they played
Are retold here and portrayed.

First Trick

Many women labor hard
Caring for a chicken yard.
Firstly, for the eggs supplied
By the worthy fowl inside.
Secondly, because a hen
Means fried chicken now and then.
Third, because their feather fluff
Is of value, too, to stuff
Squabs or pillows for one's head
(No one liking drafts in bed).—

Take Frau Bolte, here, a granny
Hating drafts as much as any.

In her yard three chickens dwell
And a lordly cock as well.—
With this state of things, what ought
One to do? the rascals thought.—
Why not get a heel of bread
(Carried out as soon as said),

Cut four equal pieces, quick,
Each a little finger thick;
These one joins with sewing thread
Length- and crosswise (one per head)
And lays out in hopes of fun

In the widow's chicken run.—
Granny's rooster at the sight
Starts to crow with all his might:

Cock-a-doodle-doo! A crumb!!
Pitter, patter, here they come.

Hens and rooster, when in reach,
Peck and swallow one bit each.

But when sense resumes its sway,
None can rightly get away.

Right and left and rear and fore,
They conduct a tug of war,

Flutter up into the air,
What a desperate affair!

Gracious me, all tangled now
And suspended from a bough!—
Their laments grow keen and keener,
And their gullets lean and leaner;

One last egg is laid apiece,
Then comes death and brings release.—

Widow Bolte from her bed
Hears the goings-on with dread.

She steps out in nameless fright
Oh, the horror of the sight!

"Flow, my tears, then, scoring, burning,
All my comfort, hope, and yearning,
All I dreamt might come to be
Dangles from this apple tree!"

Sorrow-stricken, bowed by gloom,
She has reached the place of doom,
Cuts the victims off their strings,
Lest they hang there, slack of wings,

And, despair in gait and mien,
Bears the tragic burden in.—

And was this the last trick? Wrong!
For the second won't be long.

Second Trick

As the widow on the morrow
Was reviving from her sorrow
She reflected, still distraught,
That a fine and fitting thought
Was that they (so young in years
Ravished from this vale of tears)
Should in solemn, silent pride
Be ingested, nicely fried.—
True, it brought her fresh despair
Just to see them, limp and bare,
Lie in state upon the hearth,
Who before that day of wrath,
Full of life and scratching hard,
Used to strut in walk and yard!—

Ah, once more she has to cry,
While her Spitz, bemused, stands by.—

Max and Moritz caught the scent.
"Up the roof!" their thinking went.

Through the chimney, gay and reckless,
They can see them, plump and neckless,
Browning nicely in their batter,
Grace the frying pan and spatter.—
The bereft just then repairs
To her scullery downstairs

With a ladle to scoop out
Just a dab of sauerkraut,
Which she has a passion for
When it is warmed up once more.—

Up above the fireplace
Other plans mature apace.

Max would hardly overlook
Bringing fishing rod and hook.—

Allez-oop-da! Nice and soft,
Chicken one is borne aloft.
Presto! number two and whee!
Swiftly rising, number three.
Now for number four, the last:
Easy—there! we have it fast!—
Spitz astonished, watched them soar
Bow-wow-wowing more and more.

But already thieves and prey
Have decamped and got away.—

How contentment will be shattered!
Widow B., returning, scattered
Sauerkraut and stood as rooted
When she saw the skillet looted.

Every single chicken gone!
Spitz it was she turned upon.

"Oh! Just wait, you wicked cur!!
I will have your sinful fur!!!"

And she dusted Spitz's wig
With the ladle, hard and big;
Loudly sounded his lament
As he pleaded innocent.—

Max and Moritz, though, are resting
In a shady grove, digesting.
Of the whole delicious theft
But two single legs are left.

And was this their last trick? Wrong!
For the third comes right along.

Third Trick

All the village, willy-nilly,
Knew the name of Tailor Billy.

Weekday jackets, Sunday coats,
Tapered trousers, redingotes,
Waistcoats bordered with galloons,
Woolly greatcoats, pantaloons—
Any garment, tight or loose,
Billy knew how to produce.—
Were it only darning, patching,
Shortening, perhaps, or stretching,
Or a pocket wrongly angling,
Trouser button lost or dangling—
What or where the flaw might be,
Fore or aft, to wind or lee,
He removes or remedies,
For he's pledged his life to these.—
Hence all people of the place
Show this man a pleasant face.—
Only Max and Moritz plot
How to aggravate his lot.—

Past his dwelling, one must know,
Rushing, roaring waters flow,

With a bridge of planks to guide
People to the other side.

Max and Moritz, full of spite,
Saw with mischievous delight
Reeker-rawker, heartless prank,
At the plank from bank to bank.
When the pitfall is prepared,
Loud and jeering shouts are heard:

"Bah! Come out here! Tattercoat!
Tailor, Tailor Billy-Goat!"
Almost any kind of jest
He could stand and not protest.
But when such a taunt was yelled
His immortal soul rebelled.

In one swoop he cleared the stoop,
Ell in hand: Again a whoop
Of protracted bleating smote
On his ear, and "Billy-Goat!"

He is crossing at a dash;
No! A crash, and then a splash!

Gleeful bleats and whoops, a snort—
Plop! We are a tailor short.

At this crisis of the piece
There approach a brace of geese.
Billy at his dying gasp
Seizes them with viselike clasp,

And is fluttered back to land
Shrieking goose in either hand.

What with all the stress of this,
One's physique may go amiss.

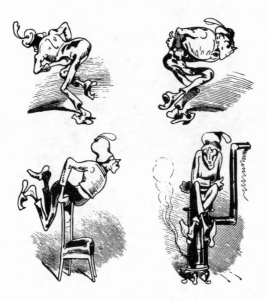

In Herr Billy's case the frolic
Netted him a painful colic.

Meet Frau Billy at her best:
For a heated iron pressed
To the belly with a will
Soon repairs the raging ill.—

Hear them up and down the street:
Billy's back upon his feet!
And was this their last trick? Wrong!
For the fourth comes right along.

Fourth Trick

From on high it is ordained
That the human mind be trained.—
Not alone the ABCs
Elevate it by degrees;
Nor does writing competence
By itself make men of sense;

Nor will 'rithmetic in season
Satisfy aspiring reason:
Moral precepts, too, are needed—
To be heard with zeal and heeded.—

Teachers see this wisely done.
Master Lampel here is one.—

Master Lampel's gentle powers
Failed with rascals such as ours;
For the evilly inclined
Pay preceptors little mind.—

Lampel, now, this worthy teacher,
Loved to smoke his pipe—a creature
Comfort which, it may be said,
Once the day's hard load is shed,
No fair-minded person can
Hold against a dear old man.—

Max and Moritz, sly as ever,
Try to think of something clever:
How to play the man a hoax
Through the meerschaum which he
    smokes.—

Once, when Sunday morning came
(Seeing him, by duty's claim,
Hard beneath the holy ceiling,
Play the organ with much feeling),
Max and Moritz tippytoed
Up into his snug abode
Where the pipe was wont to stand;
Max has seized it in his hand,

While it falls to Moritz's task
From the blasting-powder flask
To dispense a goodly gob
And to lodge it in the knob.
Out and home then at a run!
Service must be nearly done.—

Calmly, with a gentle jolt,
Lampel shot the sacred bolt,
Toils of office well discharged,
And, with key and music, barged

Off to the domestic haven,
Driven by a joyful craving

And with decorous dispatch
Stuffed his pipe and lit the match.

"Ah! to be content," he sighs,
"Is the best of earthly joys!"—

Krroom! explodes the meerschaum head
With a crash to wake the dead.

Water glass and coffeepot,
Ink, tobacco box, the lot,
Table, stove, and chair of oak,
All goes up in flash and smoke.—

Lifting fumes show him prostrated
But, thank God, still animated
By the priceless godly spark—
Though much balder now, and dark;

Hands, facade, and apertures
Are quite like a blackamoor's,
And the hair's precarious hull
Burnt away unto the skull.—
Who is now to foster youth
And diffuse scholastic truth?

Who devote such gifts as his
To his sundry offices?
How shall Teacher have a puff
With his pipe not up to snuff?—

All in course of time is mended;
But the pipe's career is ended.

And was this their last trick? Wrong!
For the fifth comes right along.

Fifth Trick

He who in his native sphere
Has an uncle living near
Must be modest and polite
To be pleasing in his sight.—
Greet him with "Good day to you!
Is there something I can do?"
Bring him journal, pipe, and spill,
And such other wants fulfill
As when, say, some twinge or twitch
In his back should pinch or itch,
Or an insect make him nervous—
Always glad to be of service.—
Or if after snuffing gently
Uncle sneezes violently,
One cries: "Bless you, Uncle dear!
May it bring long life and cheer!"—
If he enters halt of limb:
Having pulled the boots off him,
One brings slippers, gown, and lid,
Lest he shiver, God forbid.—

In a word, one tries to ease
His existence and to please.—

Max and Moritz for their part
Do not take these rules to heart.
Uncle Fritz—the coarse offense
They commit at his expense!—

Everybody knows the May
Beetle and its crawly way.
In their hundreds they will bumble
In the trees and buzz and tumble.

Max and Moritz's stratagem
Calls for quite a lot of them.

They have brought two bags of paper,
Also needed for their caper.

These they bear with catlike tread
And insert in Uncle's bed,

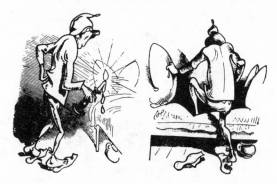

Whither he will soon repair
In his tasseled slumberwear.

In he climbs and soon is deep
In the eiderdown, asleep.

Beetles climb the featherbed
In a line for Uncle's head.

One has reached the gap and goes
Straight across to Uncle's nose.

"Fooh!" he cries, "What's up here? Ugh!"
In his hand a monster bug.

Uncle, horrified at that,
Whips out like a scalded cat.

Eek! still other beetles find
Spots above, beneath, behind;

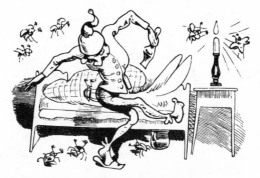

Bugs infest him, swoop, and buzz
Like some frisky, bristly fuzz.

In a frenzy Uncle Fritz
Stamps and tramples, slaps and hits.

"There! You've done, I'm telling you,
All the crawling you will do!"

Uncle, once again at rest,
Sleeps the slumber of the blest.

And was this their last trick? Wrong!
For the sixth comes right along.

Sixth Trick

Eastertime, our Savior's Passion,
Pious baker-people fashion,
Bake, adorn, and then display
Pastry work on many a tray.
Which (to see it is to love it)
Max and Moritz also covet.

But the baker, as we see,
Keeps it under lock and key,

Forcing customers to toil
Down the flue through soot and oil.

Here a pair of clients goes
Down the chimney, black as crows.

Pooff! they fall into the bin
Baker keeps the flour in.

They retrieve themselves and walk
On their way as white as chalk.

Sugared pretzels, neatly stacked,
Are the first to be attacked.

Crunch! their stairway breaks in two;

Flop! they flounder in the goo.

All encased in heavy dough,
They present a sight of woe.

Worse, the baker now discovers
And pursues the pastry lovers;

And, resourceful stratagem,
Makes two handsome loaves of them.

Good! the oven's still aglow:
Shloop! into the hole they go;

Shloop! and presently are raked
Out, for they are good and baked.—

Everyone must think they've had it;
No! they're still alive and at it!

Crisky-crusk, like mice a rusk,
They gnaw off the crispy husk.

Baker sees and hollers: Hey!!—
But they're off and clean away.—

And was this their last trick? Wrong!—
But the last comes right along!

Seventh Trick

Max and Moritz, woe is you!
For your final trick is due.—

What exactly made the two
Slit these sacks?? I wish I knew.

Here goes Farmer Klein, a sack
Full of malt-grain on his back.—

Just as he is off with it,
Grain starts leaking from the slit;

And he stops, amazed at this,
Mumbling: "Strike me! what's amiss?"

Ah! He tracks with gleeful guile
Max and Moritz in that pile.

Swoop! he scoops the worthless pack
Right into the handy sack.

Max and Moritz feel quite ill,
For this way leads to the mill.—

"Howdy, Master Miller! Hey,
Will you grind this, right away?"

"Right you are!" He dumps the lot
Down into the feeder slot.—

Rickle-rackle, rickle-rackle,
Hear the millstones grind and crackle.

Here is what the mill releases:
Still themselves, but all in pieces.

And the miller's ducks are there
To devour the loose-knit pair.

Conclusion

Those who learned this on the morrow
Gave no slightest sign of sorrow.
Widow Bolte shook her head,
Clucking: "As I always said . . ."
"Serves them right!" said Master Billy;
"Now it's they who're looking silly."
"Clearly," nodded Teacher Lampel,
"Here we have one more example!"
"Yep!" remarked the pastry cook,
"Never leap before you look."
Even Uncle Fritz said: "Hem!
Stupid jokes! For once, on them!"
This from worthy Farmer Klein:
"Ain't no business of mine . . ."
That entire place, in short,
Buzzed with joy at the report;
And they offered heartfelt thanks
For deliverance from pranks!

The Knopp Trilogy

I Adventures of a Bachelor

I Adventures of a Bachelor

Matters Reach a Crisis

Socrates, the noted sage,
Often mourned (the insight festered):
"Ah, how much is still sequestered
From the knowledge of our age!"
One thing, though, is never hidden,
For we sense it deep inside,
And it comes to us unbidden:
That we are dissatisfied.—

That's how Knopp has come to feel,
And it pains him a good deal.

His canaries in their cage
Never worry like that sage,
While Tobias feels beset
By an ill-defined regret.
Time goes by, routine grows arid;
Think, Knopp! you are still unmarried!—

True, his linen, boots, and fare
Are in Doris's faithful care;
If he needs things done or sewn
He can't get to on his own,

She is very prompt and deft
To attend him right and left.
Still and all, he's not content.—

With a wan presentiment
He consults the looking glass
For the verdict it may pass:

Viewed in front, the place looks glazed.
But in back, the Lord be praised
(He is buoyed by joyous hopes),
There should still be wooded slopes.
Oh, the penetrating sting!
There it's worse, if anything.

East to West and South to North,
Just pure reason bulges forth.

And there is another cause
For concern to give him pause:
Somehow, growing more mature,
He has passed the curvature
Drawn by Nature and decreed
Adequate unto the need
Of the center zone in question
Both for breathing and digestion.—
Nature, though, has gentle cures
For such excess curvatures:
Sip the Karlsbad waters, stalk
Flowered path and shady walk,
Exercise in rhythmic spurts,
Shun potatoes and desserts . . .
Saying to yourself "you must"
Greatly helps you to adjust.

Knopp, who feels all this acutely,

Exercises resolutely,

Sometimes musing in a clearing,

Sometimes wholly disappearing,

But returning to the spot
To resume his faithful trot.

Two whole weeks—he never fails;
Then he climbs upon the scales;
And—what does the pointer say?
Minus twenty pounds, hooray!

Onward to his second calends,
And again he mounts the balance;
What a shock! As one can see,
All is as it used to be.

In this world, he muses sadly,
There is much that functions badly,
April, cousins, maidens, May
Irretrievably decay;
And I also, soon enough,
Shall be cancelled and crossed off.
Of me too it will be read:
Knopp existed—and is dead.
Worse: will any tears be dripping
From the eye that reads the clipping?
Not a single soul will grieve
Or much notice when I leave . . .
Heads will not be sadly shaken
Where no interest is taken:
"Knopp? Who was he, anyone?"
You will hear when I am gone.
Knopp's own eyes are blinking,
    smarting . . .
At the thought of such a parting,
Of a grave untended, sere,
He himself extrudes a tear.
See it lie (commensurate
With his sorrow) where he sat.

Is this really necessary?
Shake a leg, old man, and marry!
Air yourself, get up and out,
Travel, wander, look about,
Pay some calls, you can't go wrong;
Just you see—it won't be long.

Minimal encumberments
Will be best for his intents.
Worthy Doris wipes her eyes
As she waves her fond good-byes.

An Old Flame

First, and with the least delay,
Knopp has thought to make his way
To that far idyllic vale
Which has sheltered his Adèle:

Her whose charms would so delight him
(But who did not then requite him,
Though he loved her with the whole
Of his lyrical young soul.)

He survived, as people will,
But her likeness haunts him still.
Timid, moist with perspiration,
He beholds her habitation;
Pulses pound him, tie to socks,
But at last he also knocks.

"Toby! Joy! you here at last!"
(Knopp stands riveted, aghast.)

"Here, you naughty, wayward loafer,
Sit beside me on this sofa.

You alone, my dear delight,
I have thought of day and night!
Down restraint, decorum, fashion . . .
Love me, as I love, with passion!!"
Knopp, from lack of proper feeling,
Finds his eager sweat congealing.
At this crisis in the center,
From the flank three mongrels enter.

"Help!" Adèle is heard to shout,
"Help, beloved, drive them out!"

Knopp, though, cannot see what for,
As he tiptoes to the door.—
At a run he exits there
And betakes himself elsewhere.

Clerical Help

Forward now his travels carry
Knopp on his itinerary.
To old Knarrtje (thus his name)
Warden of the local game.

As he strides along with vigor,
He observes a subfusc figure,

Which, as he is walking by,
Takes a shortcut through the rye.

Well—here comes old Knarrtje, too!
"Good old Knopp, that's nice of you!"

Chatting happily, they trudge
To the nearby keeper's lodge.

"Here—don't wait to be invited!
Why, my wife will be delighted."

But there's something to upset him.
"What the . . . Sic him, Rover, get him!

Wait, you slut . . . I never knew . . .
Let me get my hands on you!!"

Knopp's remonstrance with his host
Has no more success than most.

Hurriedly he exits there
And removes himself elsewhere.

Eggbert Nebischitz, M.A.

Now his travels carry Knopp
To the next appointed stop,
Where he hopes to spend the day
With friend Nebischitz, M.A.

Nebischitz, though not quite done
With a lesson to his son,

On perceiving his old friend
Gladly brings it to an end,

And prepares to do his best
For the comfort of his guest:
"Mark, my Kuno! Swiftly flit
Where I order you, to wit
(Listen well): Betake yourself
Cellarwards, where on a shelf
Wrapped in straw upon a trestle
Some Bordeaux is found to nestle.
This Bordeaux, I charge you, fetch
And deliver with dispatch."

Kuno, suitably equipped,
Gladly hurries to the crypt,

Where he quietly diverts
Some invigorating squirts
Down his esophageal chasm;
And a world of good it does him.

The resulting short supply
He replenishes nearby.

Claret is for men of wits
One of life's prime benefits.

Seldom is a glass declined.
Knopp, however, makes a find.

"From its shape one might infer
Pigeon droppings . . . as it were.

Kuno, tell me if you can
What has caused this—man to man!"

Having probed to Kuno's core,
He desists and pours some more.

And his friend responds . . . In vain:
Foreign matter, once again.

"Well, now—this, I would have sworn,
Is a sparrow, newly born.

Kuno!! Tell me if you can
What has caused this—man to man!!
Your transgressions' inky maze
Lies transparent to my gaze.

Go! my trust has been abused.
Leave my sight. You are . . . excused!"
Eggbert's rule has ever been:
Caning merely skims the skin;
Only reason's scalpel can
Penetrate the inner man.

Knopp decides to exit there
And remove himself elsewhere.

Bucolic Entertainment

Now his travels carry Knopp
On to yet another stop.
To a dear old friend he came
In the country, Ruff by name.

Ruff has always thought a skinful
Salutary for the sinful.
And a sterling medicine
In advance of any sin.
Prior to the village dance
He applies it to his Franz.

Knopp can hear while still remote
The familiar plaintive note.

Then all four proceed in state
To the local marksmen's fête.

Francis has discreetly snatched
A curvaceous tail, detached,
As he has been well aware,
From a pig just slaughtered there.

Soon the guest's bipartite stern
Takes a most amusing turn.

Presently the French horn brays
For the opening Française.

None, the company agrees,
Match our Knopp in grace and ease,

Or contrives like him to sway
To the tune and swoop away.

But a magic all his own
Works when he performs alone.

Everyone is quite uplifted,
Finding Knopp so greatly gifted.
Soon, alas, the tunes subside,
And with pardonable pride

Here the star returns to base

For a drink and change of pace.

Oops! there is no base at all.
Knopp sustains a grievous fall.

His recovery is fleet
But, he senses, incomplete.

For, aghast, he feels abaft
An unseasonable draft.

Rapidly he exits there
And betakes himself elsewhere.

Pastorale

Knopp's sartorial default
Brings his progress to a halt.

For this lonesome, flowery mead
Answers his undoubted need

Of a dry dock, as it were,
For inspection and repair;

Just the haven, it would seem,
To restore one's self-esteem

After recent bare escapes.
Just a baby rabbit gapes.

Here comes farmer Reuben. Rightly
Knopp conceals himself, but lightly.

But with Reuben's consort, Susie,
He becomes a lot more choosy.

Now they vanish up the lea,
And directly Knopp is free
To devote his full concern
To his lacerated stern.—
He attends to it, becalmed,
When once more he is alarmed

By an imminent—oh, Hades!
Troop of promenading ladies.
Here they are! Of Knopp, though, phew!

Just the top remains in view.

First a gasp of petrifaction,
Then the governess takes action,

Pealing loudly: "O mon Dieu!
C'est un homme! Fermez les yeux!!"

Flustered by his near escape,
Knopp resumes his social shape

And forsakes this Central Station
For another destination.

Bubbelmann

On again his travels carry
Knopp on his itinerary;

To another friend he came
(Bubbelmann his charming name),

Whom he knew as bright and hearty,
Life and soul of any party.

He emerges. "Happy day!"
Burbles Knopp, "I've come to stay!"

Bubbelmann, benign but pale,
Answers: "Worthy brother, hail!

Firstly: lodgement for the night
Would not seem to be in sight,
For a churchman of renown
Has arrived from out of town.

Second, as to boarding here,
There is little hope, I fear:
First day, we are born afresh,
Second day, we kill the flesh,
Third day, purge the soul of dross,
Fourth day, walk beneath the Cross.

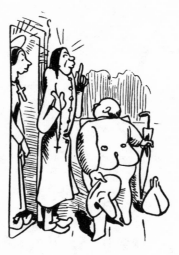

On the last and saddest score . . .
Hush! my wife is at the door!"

Disconcerted by all this,
Knopp, while wishing loads of bliss,
Turns his back upon these two,
Bidding them a cool adieu.

Swiftly exiting from there,
He betakes himself elsewhere.

Enough Is Less Than a Feast

Knopp on his peregrination
Reached the next appointed station;
To a worthy friend he came,
Sexton Plünne was his name.

Coming through the gate, he sees
Shirts aflutter in the breeze;
Whence he gathers right away:
It's the Plünnes' washing day.

And for added confirmation,
There's old Plünne's occupation.

Gladly, though, he frees his lap,
Crying: "Welcome, Knopp, old chap!

Hold the baby while I find
Dinner for us—would you mind?"

This is something new to Knopp.
Plünne clears the tabletop.

Knopp feels more and more unable,
While the sexton sets the table.

Now he dives into a pouch
In the matrimonial couch,
And it opens to the sheen
Of a handsome soup tureen.

Insulators of renown—
None compare with eiderdown.—
Now, if dinner, for example,
Has been relatively ample,
And the children, duly cautioned,
Had their seconds strictly portioned,
Leaving loads of tripe, or oodles
(As the case may be) of noodles,

It is plainly for the best
That one should conserve the rest
As a hot and wholesome saving
In the parents' downy haven,
So when shades of evening climb
Supper's ready in no time.

Plünne, here, has all along
Kept this custom, right or wrong.

"Now," says Plünne, "if you will,
Sit with us and eat your fill!"
Knopp has lost his appetite
And resorts to sudden flight.

Hastily he exits there
And betakes himself elsewhere.

Friend Klaeppi

On his further travels Knopp
Came to yet another stop,
Where he called upon a chappie
By the merry name of Klaeppi.

Anyone can see how happy
Klaeppi is with Mrs. Klaeppi.

With a tenderness which pleases
He embraces her and breezes:
"Well, dear, for the nonce, good-bye!
We're invited, Knopp and I,

To the Antiquaries' Club
For a lecture and some grub."

It appears the learned gathering's
Round the corner from St. Catherine's
In a cozy little place
Called the Merry Boniface.

Klaeppi seems no stranger there.
He bespeaks some wholesome fare.

Cockerels and breaded fishes
Both are admirable dishes;

With it? Excellent proposal!
Quite! A lively little Mosel.

After which, a sparkling Rhône . . . ?
Sine qua . . . ? Precisely—*non*!

Good! They're joined by Resi, who
Will accept a glass or two.

"Well, now—all good things must end!
Would you mind . . . the bill, old friend?"

Presently, the two are swaying
To the inn where Knopp is staying.

True, it's late, but—how absurd!
They can't make their presence heard.

Klaeppi waves: "Who cares?" says he.
Come and stay the night with me."

What with one thing and another,
Finding keyholes is a bother.

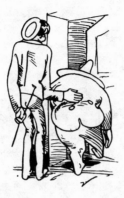

"There, it's open . . . After you!
Enter, friend, and pass right through."

Knopp complies. But canny Klaeppi
Temporizes, looking happy.

Then, with no alert at all,
Knopp is pinned against the wall.

"Got you!" Mrs. Klaeppi cries.
"Antiquaries . . . stuff and lies!"

All in darkness, and unhappy,
She's confusing him with Klaeppi.

Wheee! how Knopp is brought to grips
As the besom pokes and whips!

Shlop! he shelters, more or less,
In some tub of nastiness.

Ouch! the broom's no longer whole,
And the center is all pole.

In a damp, amorphous clutter
Knopp is swept into the gutter.

Hurriedly he exits there
And betakes himself elsewhere.

Happy Event

Onward his migrations carry
Knopp on his itinerary;
To a valued friend he came,
Sourdough was his curious name.

Sourdough, full of bouncy cheer,
Has just spiked and mulled some beer.

"Yoicks!" he yodels, "Step inside!
Hip hurray! My wife just died!

Look: beneath the candles here
She reposes on a bier.

Now she can't butt in on us . . .
Come, sit down and have a glass;

Down the hatch, and take the pledge:
Never tumble off that edge!
Marriage squeezes, let me own,
Tears and money from a stone:

Pay for curlers, girdles, bras,
Novels, fashion journals, spas,
Buy new dresses, silk-lined capes,
Concert tickets, window drapes—
Chatter, natter, nag and pout . . .
Bottoms up! She's down . . . I'm out!"

"Be not downhearted,
Morning dawns bright;
Troubles departed
Count for delight."

There, a creak, the door uncloses—
And who issues? Holy Moses!

His lamented, who had suffered
From some seizure, has recovered!!

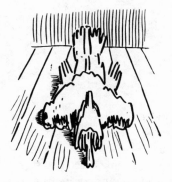

Salted, like the wife of Lot,
He is dead now, she is not.

Knopp is leaving, *ventre-à-terre*,
To betake himself elsewhere.

Oh, No . . .

Knopp once more has come to rest
On his self-appointed quest;
To an older friend he came,
Pippo was his handy name.

Laughter, bell-like voices tolling:
Pippo with his daughters, strolling . . .

"This dear fellow, is my Hilda.
Here the elder is Clotilda.
Hilda's bridal party's due
In the morning, twelve to two.
But Clotilda, I may state,
Still is fancy-free to date.

Ah—the balmy eventide . . .
Knopp and Tilda, side by side . . .
Tilda plucks a rose for him;
And he senses, deep within:
"Knopp, this moment you were blessed°
With the answer to your quest!"

Soon by Pippo he is guided
Where his couch has been provided.
"This big dining room we borrow
For the big affair tomorrow.

Over here you find the spot
Set apart for you-know-what.

And your room is opposite.
Have a restful night in it!"

Knopp's sweet fancies, all awhirl,
Dance about that slender girl,
And he presses, lips apart,
Her dear rose against his heart.
"Oh, Clotilda, you alone
Shall and must become my own."—

Then he feels an inner pleading
For a little quiet reading.—
And why not? He takes the paper
And proceeds with rose and taper
Straight across the empty hall
To obey the harmless call.
Sitting, reading, like enough
You get drowsy and nod off.

It's next morning, rather late
After sunrise, seven or eight—
Peals of merry girlish laughter
Echoing from wall and rafter:
It's the bridesmaids' busy throng,
Who have been astir quite long
Decorating and adorning
Doors and walls this festive morning.—
"I can't spend all day in here!"
Quavers Knopp in stark despair,

And, well camouflaged, he streams
From the locus of his dreams
Like a rushing wind on legs;

But the threshold rudely pegs
All advance—his fall is fated.
Gosh . . . ! He is defoliated.

Secretly he exits there
And betakes himself elsewhere.

Warning from on High

Knopp ascends in headlong flight
Up a rugged mountain height.

In a stark and craggy glen
He detects a hermit's den.

Now the hermit, hoar and sere,
Issues from the crevice here
And from the old gladstone's wattle
Gravely lifts the brandy bottle.

"I am Krökel," he intones,
And I loathe all worldly drones.

All below is dross and swill.
Many thanks, I think I will.

Oh, you sponges, brushes, combs,
Body lotions, shaving foams,
Grooming aids and eyebrow tweezers,
Eyelash teasers, pimple squeezers,
Shirt-and-tie and breeches, pooh!
Krökel scorns the lot of you.

All is dross to me and swill.
Many thanks—I think I will.

Phew, you women! Pshaw, you girls!
Legs and torsos, bumps and curls,

Glances luring, bottoms inching,
Fingers amorously pinching,
All your frills and folderol,
Krökel execrates it all.

All is stench to me and swill.
Many thanks, I think I will.

But to Her, in halos golden,
Only Her, I feel beholden,
Thee alone I worship, love,
Unattainable above,
Thee, my lovely, ever far
Blessèd Emerentia.

All the rest is rot and swill.
Many thanks, I think I will.

Here the holy hermit yaws
Over backwards. Knopp withdraws.—
Knopp reflects: this anchorite
Was a pretty loathsome sight,
And long-distance mooning, roundly
Said, depresses me profoundly.

And he leaves this cheerless spot
At a dogged homeward trot.

Return and Conclusion

Knopp's return is swift and steady.
Here he is, at home already.

Heaving to behind the billows
Of his Doris, smoothing pillows,

"Wench," he stammers, "if I were . . ."
And she smiles: "With pleasure, Sir!"

Soon a modest printed head
Frames the two as duly wed:

Tobias Knopp
Dorothea Lickyfat

First by dry official motion
Then with fervor and devotion.

There—at peace at last and certain . . .
Whoosh! Young Cupid draws the curtain.

Clement Dove,

THE POET THWARTED

First Chapter

I envy people who can pen
A pretty poem now and then.

Congenitally shrewd and clever,
Man recognizes, now as ever,
That much contrariness and woe
Besets him daily here below.
Joy is capricious and elusive,
Annoyance blatant and obtrusive.
One goes about all glum and dank,
His buttonhole so void and blank;
Another feels that life is blighted
Because his love is unrequited.
Perplexities dog every stride;
And one that cannot be denied,
The worry how to make ends meet,
Keeps us forever on our feet.
A hearty "How are you" will quickly
Make most of us feel somewhat sickly;
We manage but a feeble glow
And mumble "Oh, so-so, you know . . ."
Avoid the lying hypocrite
Who yodels "Splendid! Very fit!"
For by and large, we spend our days
In vague discomfort and malaise.

Not so the bard. For hardly palls
The dreary sight of his four walls,
When, presto, he has struck and furled
The moldy backdrops of our world,
And issues from its gloom and tension
Into the poets' fifth dimension.
(The fourth is full of cosmic mists
And rank with ghosts and physicists.)

Here is the realm of light and buoyance,
Here he is rid of all annoyance,
Here from the boundless-bosomed Muses
The priceless stuff forever oozes
For him to gather and decant
To his hygienic dairy plant.
The honest dairywife each day
Creates fresh butter just this way.
The first to rise, the last to drowse,
She tugs between the legs of cows
With cunning wrists, astride a stool;
And what comes out, she sets to cool
On shelves, where soon with finger bent
She skims the fatty element,
Collects it in a mighty urn,
Rolls up her sleeves and starts to churn.
Long with the perforated brass
She worries the elusive mass.
It squelches, squooshes, gulps and goops,
Leaps up and down in tortured loops,
Until the substance, tickled sick,
Disintegrates in thin and thick.
And now she reaps the rich return:
She lifts the thick stuff from the churn,
She works and plies it, kneads and tucks;
At last she reverently plucks
With tender fingers from the mold
The cake of butter, plump and gold.
Just so the poet. All devout,
He's squeezed and sweated something out
And eyes with pleasure and respect
The product of his intellect.
But an unselfish man desires
To share the things that he admires.
The author with his precious freight
Is not at ease, he cannot wait,
He savors neither work nor leisure
Until he can display his treasure

To kindred souls. He goes to look,
He finds a friend, by hook or crook,
And him, although he gently strains,
He unavoidably detains
And steers, as for a quiet harbor,
To some secluded bench or arbor
By one lapel or button vital
To offer him a free recital.
And there we are: Like magic issues
With crackles of unfolding tissues
From the recesses of his dress
A most voluminous MS.
His eyes grow bright, his gestures rampant,
The listener gets a little dampened,
For close and hot like pipes of Pan
He feels the impact of the man.
"Superb!" the poet's friend may say;
(The author's view, in every way.)

To credit what is clear as light
Is surely everybody's right.
What sweet fulfilment, when the find
By him discovered, shaped, and mined,
His sparkling spirit's graceful caper,
Is printed in the morning paper
And early at the dewy dawn
Delivered to the porch or lawn!
The hiss of steaming kettles rouses
The sleepyheads in all the houses,
Grandma and parents, youths and girls
With shining teeth and glistening curls
Sit down to coffee, eggs, and toast
And one by one peruse the *Post*;
And each in turn has panegyrics
For our poet's charming lyrics.
Up soars the verse and forthwith passes
Through their pince-nez or other glasses;
Past lense and retina it darts
Into the readers' brains and hearts.
Its vagrant lilt, its sinuous vowels,
They liquefy the very bowels,
They percolate to every cell
Of persons subject to the spell.
Thenceforward, deep in their insides,
Encompassed snugly by their hides
And by the divers outer covers,
The poet wafts his balm and hovers,
Until at last he is depleted,
Absorbed, exuded, or excreted.
A happy fate! But should it bore him,
A happier yet is still before him.
For Beatrice, his lady fair,
His *femme fatale*, his sweet despair,
Who tortured him with distant charms,
Now nestles glowing in his arms
And breathes: "It's me! Like, your admirer!
D'you do that pome in the *Enquirer*?

I really was RELATING to it!
It beats me, honest, how you do it!"

I envy people with this brand
Of poetry at their command.

Second Chapter

A gentle clerk named Clement Dove
Was well aware of the above.
Not that he feels deprived or harried.
He has a job, and he is married.

Four healthy children, too, all told,
Are his to cherish and to hold.
And yet he feels, for all his bliss,
That deep down something is amiss.
He yearns to write, to speak with tongues,
He wants to blossom forth in songs
That strike a chord in every man.
He feels he must, and therefore can.

Seized by the drive, his mind a hive,
He leaves his office after five

And seeks the Park, to woo the Muse
In those congenial purlieus.

One who, like him, is darkly fraught
With images, and great with thought,
Needs for his consecrated labors
A place to sit, away from neighbors.

But all the benches are encumbered
With parties odd- or even-numbered.
One might do better to repair
Where beer is served in open air.

Among the seats set out for drinking
He picks one suitable for thinking.

The waiting girl's proximity
Disturbs his equanimity,

But soon a noble draft of grain
Uplifts him to a higher plane.
A genial glow warms head and rear . . .
By Jove! A marvellous idea!

Quick for the phrase to bring it out!
Alas, it does not come about.

Just as the pen begins to fly,
Dove's hat descends on ear and eye.
A friend who has this type of mind
Thought thus to greet him from behind.

Dove leaves enraged and out of trim.
The friend drinks up his beer for him.

Arrived, he hangs his coat and hat
Upon the tree on hand for that

And gets down from another bracket
His soft beret and smoking jacket,
Which grace the poet when at home
As rhyme and meter grace the po'm.

He paces with a somber frown,
Now looking up, now looking down.

There slowly ripens in his brain
The rhythm of the first quatrain.

The doorbell shrill dispels the thrill.
Here comes his lady with a bill.
She warbles to him: "Clement dear,
I have to bother you, I fear.
The cobbler's boy is at the door.
He says we owe ten-twenty-four."
With special venom one resents
Pecuniary botherments.

Now let us hope he beats the jinx.
He stands by his *prie-dieu* and thinks

"O vision graceful and appealing!"
Enraptured he adjures the ceiling.

This time the door bursts even wider:

"Dad, you're the horse and we're the rider!
Come on, we're carrying the mail,
And Indians are on our trail!
Whoa, let me get up on his rump.
Now jump, you lazy pony, jump!

Oh giddyup! Hey, little Jim,
You'd better lay the whip on him!"
No loosely anchored compositions
Can gain a hold in such conditions.—
A man so circumstanced who might
Conjecture that the dead of night
Should be conducive, inter alia,
To lucid thought, is in for failure.
Papa has just gone on to bed.
His feet grow warm, and in his head
There starts that incandescent glow . . .
Someone goes Waah!, at first quite low,
But one Waah always wakes another.
Soon the whole room is in a pother.
From Mama's mouth a strident hissing
Supplies a part that has been missing;
And last, beneath the overtones
Chimes in the bass of Papa's groans.
A father's feelings at this stage
No bachelor can ever gauge.

Third Chapter

An intellectual in a pinch
Acts, while a lesser man would flinch.
Dove realizes that his power
Needs but the quiet place and hour
To catalyze in calm seclusion
The tranquil growth, the final fusion.
Thus diagnosticates his mind:
Leave this environment behind!
Retire to a rustic scene,
Where life is pleasant and serene,
Where Nature stills all haste and passion,
And Virtue is not out of fashion!

Poets are apt to travel light:
A Gladstone bag, embroidered bright,
Is trim and does not take much packing.
A little hat should not be lacking.
A campstool, notebook, bow-tie spruce,
Soft-collared shirt a little loose,
A Faber pencil sharp and yellow,
And last not least, the old umbrello.

Seen off by all the family,

He cries: "Good-bye, dear Emily!
I'll think of you among the peasants
And bring you back some lovely presents!"
With this he makes on wingèd feet
For a bohemian's third-class seat.

With hoot and hiss, with clank and cough
The little engine potters off.

First slow, then swiftly flitted past,
By wires interknitted fast,
The dour and dull fraternal souls
Of countless telegraphic poles.

Those fanning fields and whirling fences
Are apt to stupefy the senses
And turn the spirit back inside.
The undulations of the ride,
The gentle sway and rhythmic tremble
Help thoughts to waken and assemble;

And some that might have meant to hover
Just out of range, are flushed from cover.

At length to Clement's mind appears
A brace of exquisite ideas.—

Here is his stop! The whistle toots.
A countryman in hobnailed boots

Now enters like a buffalo
And throws his weight on Clement's toe.

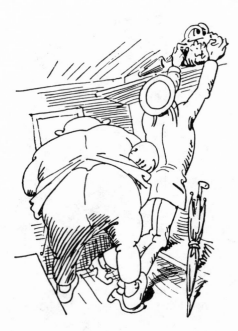

The bloom of youth, it fades and wanes.
A corn remains.
We know the symptoms well enough:
The lips are pursed, as though to puff;
The limbs grow stiff, the eyes are closed,
Some curled-up nerve ends are exposed.
The subject as a whole is glued
In an eccentric attitude.

This ritual posture of distress
Does not afford the least redress.
But any witness of one's plight
Seems much the better for the sight.

Fourth Chapter

How blithely in the noonday haze
The little hamlet meets the gaze!

The poet, bothered by a blister,
Welcomes the unpretentious vista.

Here on his horsie little Art
Rides through a puddle, bless his heart.

There in the barnyard, blunt and young,
Stands Ebenezer in the dung.
His mood serene, his stance superb,
He scents the air with homely herb.

The honest churl admires Pearl,
The pert and buxom hired girl.
She keeps the goatshed nice and clean;
And peace enfolds the rustic scene.

In modest quarters of his choice
Dove listens for Apollo's voice.
Inhaling deeply, he admires
The placid view, the sunset's fires;
He listens to the pensive knells

Of vesper and of cattle bells;
And presently the Delphic lyre
Strikes up and touches him with fire.

Kerplunk! Above the pink geranium
Intrudes a huge and hornèd cranium.
With evil breath and muzzle spread,
It trumpets fit to wake the dead.
The poem's graceful counterpoint
Is jarred and shattered out of joint.

Let poets hide when Nature sings!
The singer exits through the wings.

Fifth Chapter

The morning dawned; the sun arose.
Is Dove restored by sweet repose?
Dost know the tiny fiend with wings
That flits about the nose and sings?
Dost also know that other batch,
Quite wingless, but as hard to catch?

Take a good look at Clement's map.
Don't ask, just pity the poor chap.

Beneath the flowering lilac here,
Clement has settled with his gear.

Behind him, where the fence is rent,
Young Arthur loiters with intent.

He arms his horsie with a stinger
And evidently means to linger.
He starts committing hostile acts
His victim misconstrues the facts.

Suspecting a mosquito bite,
He claps his hand upon the site.

He pauses to inspect the haul.
Perhaps it wasn't one at all.

But hardly has he found it so,
When he is punctured from below.

This makes the poet somewhat warier.
More strength is needed in this area.

So down again, and that was that.
Now let us—Oops! there goes his hat.

"A breeze," he mutters with a frown,
Retrieves his hat and pulls it down.

Still unsuspecting, he resumes
His seat, or rather, he assumes
The stance, and takes the seat for granted.
No wonder he is disenchanted.

The stool is snatched away. He settles
Into a thicket full of nettles.

This is conclusive evidence!
A joker lurks behind this fence
The thing to do with such a chap
Is to play dumb and lay a trap.

He stoops again and sits in wait,
A tempting overhang for bait.

The stick is quick, but he is quicker;
His timing could not have been slicker.

The reasoner was not misled.
He hit the nail upon the head.

Dove skips about and sheds some blood.

Young Art regains his native mud.

Sixth Chapter

Most men of letters like a date
With Nature in her virgin state.
The gentle folds of flowering heaths
Invite to saunter, braiding wreaths
Of buttercups and dandelions.
One wanders through the scented pines,
Glad to renounce for Nature's essence
All architectural excrescence.

Here Clement dallies in a trance,
Devoutly raising limbs and glance.
He feels the world is vast and blue
Especially in upward view.

But isolationist and shrinking
Remains the earwig's way of thinking.

Deaf to creation's joyous chord,
It clambers meanly through the sward.
To feel protected, snug, and smug
Is all that matters to the bug.

Seen from the viewpoint of a boarder,
The poet's ear looks made to order;
That close and gloomy shelter seems
Ideal for sleep, perchance for dreams . . .

But if it thinks a long career
Is yet vouchsafed to it down here,
It errs.—A swipe of Clement's shoe
With energetic follow-through

Destroys, but for a scrambled rest,
The shape peculiar to this pest;
And as an independent agent,
It disappears from Nature's pageant,
Thus proving it no pass to bliss
To crawl and mind one's business.
Forthwith, and at a lively pace,
Our friend relinquishes this place
For a more elevated perch
Atop a knoll, beneath a birch.

A bird skips overhead and trills.
The poet's soul expands and thrills.
Fresh glories swim into his ken.
His genius crackles in the pen.

Whiz-ping! Oh ding! A shocking thing.
Relieved, the little bird takes wing.

And likewise the terrestrial singer
Has just decided not to linger.

The sky, at first but lightly clouded,
Now lowers ominously shrouded.
A little rain is safely shed
By an umbrella fully spread.

Ungainly and of little use
Is an umbrella with a sluice.

Across the meadow, fast and lithe,
Strides Ebenezer with a scythe.
The gust and rain obscure his view.
Dove's canopy is slit in two.

But this will not cause Dove to flinch,
Who kept his head by half an inch.
What's more, the rain-cloud has receded,
And shelter is no longer needed.

Dove strolls downhill a little while
And meets young Pearl atop a stile.

He stops in passing, half in jest,
And tries to fasten at her breast
A playful flowery caress—
(The Poet and The Shepherdess).

A slap strikes home like thunderclap.

A fall compounds the sad mishap.

What fools men be! They stand perplexed,
Look sheepish or a little vexed,

Instead of calling upon Science
To solve the thing by ergs or ions.
There swells a cheek, all lush and free.
Here hangs a hand. Add Energy.
Now, by the secret operation
Of extra-physical causation,
This Energy, at first but latent,
Becomes kinetically patent.
It yanks the hand up like a streak
And turns to Heat along the cheek.
This heat is carried by the nerves
Through many complex twists and curves

To a compartment in the brain,
Where the effect is felt as Pain.

(Thermodynamics, ch. 3.)
A clouted ear to you and me.

Seventh Chapter

The Moon. O name so apt and round,
Of soft, insinuating sound!
Who could be so invidious,
So callous, cold, and hideous
As not to have his heartstrings stirred
To gentle tremors at the word?

The hamlet in the moonlight gleams;
The peasants dream their hoggish dreams;
In slumber wrapped are man and brute,
Alone the watchman has to toot,
Because his office brooks no dozing;
But Clement, moonstruck, is composing . . .

What signal is this from the stable?
It's Pearl who beckons from the gable!

She evidently feels remorse
For having been so rude and coarse.
The poet, who is not a boor,
Accepts the tender overture.

He climbs, by way of some manure,
Through a restricted aperture.

Hullo? A harsh and scornful bleating
Is a most unexpected greeting.

The charge comes with a single grunt.
The author's pelvis bears the brunt.

A two-pronged thrust that hurts and vexes
Strikes home about the solar plexus.

A hamper offers welcome shelter.
The poet takes it, helter-skelter.

The wickerwork is sound and tough.
The point is, is it deep enough?
All of a sudden, Pearl is here
With her devoted cavalier;
She carries mischief in her soul,
And he a sturdy wooden pole.

He threads it through the hamper's eyes
Between the inmate's weaving thighs;
And thus uncomfortably grooved,
Dove feels himself picked up and moved.

He struggles hotly, for profound
Yawns the dark query: Whither bound?

A well-spring, moonlit, deep and cool
Awaits the swaying reticule.

Here they proceed to dunk the basket
More frequently than Dove would ask it.

Their hamper tipped and shaken clean,

The rustic lovers leave the scene.

Eighth Chapter

What boots it to defy the tide,
If just one's feet remain outside?

To Dove, besides chagrin and choler,
It booted a neuralgic molar.

A toothache, not to be perverse,
Is an unmitigated curse,
Except for one redeeming feature:
That it compels the stricken creature
To marshal all those vital forces
It used to spend on drink and horses
And bring them into proper focus
Upon a single inner locus.
The pain is hardly on the job
With that premonitory throb,
And fare ye well, embattled nations,
Forgotten are those stock quotations,
Deadlines, deductions, yearly giving;
The pattern of accustomed living
That once was palpable and plain
Seems insubstantial now and vain.
One does not like one's coffee hot,
All auld acquaintance is forgot,
For in one tooth a paltry hole
Comprises the immortal soul,
And with each purgatory bout
Grows the resolve: Let's have it out!

Before we write another date,
The poet has attained this state.

Shot through with anguish to the core,
He fumes at Dr. Pocket's door.

Projected from his cozy nest,
The doctor heeds the bell's behest.
He does not mind Dove's urgencies.
In fact, he likes emergencies.

He cries: "How do you do, dear Sir?
Won't you be seated? In this chair!

Now let us see—what have we here?"
(The finger tastes a little queer.)

"Ah yes. Quite so. Looks pretty black.
Now just relax and settle back!

Heave-ho!!
How was it? Did you feel it shift?"
"I certainly felt something lift."

"In that case there is nothing to it!
Another little tug will do it!

Heeaa—ve-ho!!!"
He prises with a hamlike paw.

The tooth stays rooted in the jaw.

"I thought as much," says Dr. Pocket.

"The obstacle is in the socket.
Five dollars net is all you owe.

I hope it passes. Let me know!"

Ninth Chapter

True, lyric bards must pay their toll
In noble anguish of the soul;
But Clement's proletarian hurt
Contributes little to convert
A singer without rank or name
Into a laureate of fame.
Above, a scowl; below, a growl;
A kerchief frames the swollen jowl.
He now detests rusticity,
With little Art's duplicity,
With Pearl's insidious perjury,
And Dr. Pocket's surgery,
The cows, the bugs, the yokels' smirks,
The whole insipid footling works,
And hears his martyred molar nag:
Oh, let's go home! (First pack your bag.)

He would have liked to reach the station
Without a noisy demonstration.

As it turns out, he must endure
A final small discomfiture.
Crude imitations of a bleat
Accompany him down the street;
The very goat behind her door
Remembers that they met before.
A guileless city man who read it
Would probably refuse to credit
How fast such information flows.
The countryman will nod. He knows.

When Dove at last has caught the train,
He feels some respite from the strain.
A mother and a wicker bag
With baby's bottle and a rag

Companion the exhausted tripper.
The infant is alert and chipper.
It waves and kicks its chubby limbs,
Its rosy muzzle overbrims,
It's such a precious little nugget,
A bachelor might want to hug it.
Oh-oh! The sunny mood departs.
Mama solicitously starts
To pipe to him his travel ration.

But he rejects it in a passion,
And with no civilized restraints
He trumpets long and strident plaints.
The milk is cold! It's not his fault.
Oh good! The train comes to a halt.
"Could you just hold him on your arm?
I'll run and get his bottle warm!"
She races to the restaurant place.
The train, one fears, will win the race.

Tooot . . . All aboard! They spring the trap.
The wailing baby on his lap,
With throbbing tooth and swollen cheek,
Dove sways along in soot and reek
Toward his own, his native station.
At five they reach his destination.
The tot, worn out by his alarms,
Rests warm and still in Clement's arms;
And yet the hope swells very large
To place him in official charge.

The guard to whom the find is brought
Declines to entertain the thought.

So does the master of the station.

So does the man at Information.
To take the foundling home to stay
Seems for the nonce the only way.

Homeward the weary wanderer fares.
Four happy children line the stairs.
"Come, children," Mother says, "let's see,
What can that great big present be?"

But when the burden meets her eyes,
She does not relish the surprise.

"Clement!!" she falters, "take it back!!"
Then everything around goes black.

The infant's mother intervenes,
Forestalling more distressing scenes.
The bottle once again is cold,
But he is in no mood to scold.

With hasty thanks the guests depart.
Dove does not take it much to heart.
Most men are gladly separated
From infants who are not related.

Conclusion

Now Dove lays down his aching head.
His loving wife tucks him in bed.

His bulbousness begins to wane.
Soft waves of sleep assuage the pain

And bring a dream of joyous calm.
His soul is soothed as with a balm
Of indescribable delight.
There shimmers in his dazzled sight
A lady, snowy-draped and winged,
Her feet by rosy vapors ringed.
She smiles and beckons to enfold
Her hand, be wafted off . . . Behold—
Most natural of wondrous things—
He too has grown a pair of wings

And starts aloft with outspread hands
To soar with her to other lands.
But oh! A thrill of nameless dread;
With viselike clutch and tons of lead
Reality and all her minions
Encumber his unfolding pinions

And halt the rapturous ascent.
By demon bleats the air is rent.
The sweet celestial vision wanes,
And only one stark fact remains—

His lady's voice at ten past eight:
"Wake up, my pet! It's getting late!"
At nine he passes through his door
Bound for the office as before.

Thus fades all glamorous illusion
Before the obvious conclusion:
The obstacles are always small;
One mustn't get involved, that's all.

Gedichte

Mein Lebenslauf

Mein Lebenslauf ist bald erzählt.—
In stiller Ewigkeit verloren
Schlief ich, und nichts hat mir gefehlt,
Bis daß ich sichtbar ward geboren.
Was aber nun?—Auf schwachen Krücken,
Ein leichtes Bündel auf dem Rücken,
Bin ich getrost dahingeholpert,
Bin über manchen Stein gestolpert,
Mitunter grad, mitunter krumm,
Und schließlich mußt ich mich verschnaufen.
Bedenklich rieb ich meine Glatze
Und sah mich in der Gegend um.
Oweh! Ich war im Kreis gelaufen,
Stand wiederum am alten Platze,
Und vor mir dehnt sich lang und breit,
Wie ehedem, die Ewigkeit.

Poems

Curriculum Vitae

My life? There isn't much to tell.
In still eternity forlorn
I slumbered, all at ease and well,
Till rendered visible and born.
What followed? Down a knobbly track,
A flimsy bundle on my back,
I lightly marched through field and wood,
Now on the crook, now on the straight;
At last I settled on the grass
To catch my breath. I scratched my pate,
I scrutinized the neighborhood:
I'd come full circle—yes, alas!
Back to the place where I had stood,
And far and wide in front of me
There ranged, as then, eternity.

Walter Arndt

Ach, ich fühl es! Keine Tugend
Ist so recht nach meinem Sinn;
Stets befind ich mich am wohlsten,
Wenn ich damit fertig bin.

Dahingegen so ein Laster,
Ja, das macht mir viel Pläsier;
Und ich hab die hübschen Sachen
Lieber vor als hinter mir.

Die Liebe war nicht geringe.
Sie wurden ordentlich blaß;
Sie sagten sich tausend Dinge
Und wußten noch immer was.

Sie mußten sich lange quälen,
Doch schließlich kam's dazu,
Daß sie sich konnten vermählen.
Jetzt haben die Seelen Ruh.

Bei eines Strumpfes Bereitung
Sitzt sie im Morgenhabit;
Er liest in der Kölnischen Zeitung
Und teilt ihr das Nötige mit.

Wer möchte diesen Erdenball
Noch fernerhin betreten,
Wenn wir Bewohner überall
Die Wahrheit sagen täten.

Ihr hießet uns, wir hießen euch
Spitzbuben und Halunken,
Wir sagten uns fatales Zeug
Noch eh wir uns betrunken.

Sad to say, there's not a virtue
I can ever have much fun with;
Always I am at my easiest
When that business is done with.

Quite conversely, it is vices
That agree with me, I find:
Pleasant little jobs I'd rather
See before me than behind.

Walter Arndt

Their love was ever unsated,
They all but wasted away;
A thousand things they debated
And always had more to say.

Long years they were baulked and harried,
But time provided release;
They had their way and were married,
And now at last are at peace.

She sits there, loosely appareled,
Creating some bedroom shoes;
He studies the Morning Herald
And gives her the gist of the news.

Walter Arndt

Who would be brave enough to dwell
On earth and walk his rut
If all of us resolved to tell
The truth and nothing but?

Then names would swarm on busy wings
Like scoundrel, hoodlum, skunk,
We'd tell each other awful things
Before we're even drunk.

Und überall im weiten Land,
Als langbewährtes Mittel,
Entsproßte aus der Menschenhand
Der treue Knotenknittel.

Da lob ich mir die Höflichkeit,
Das zierliche Betrügen.
Du weißt Bescheid, ich weiß Bescheid;
Und allen macht's Vergnügen.

Wirklich, er war unentbehrlich!
Überall, wo was geschah
Zu dem Wohle der Gemeinde,
Er war tätig, er war da.

Schützenfest, Kasinobälle,
Pferderennen, Preisgericht,
Liedertafel, Spritzenprobe,
Ohne ihn, da ging es nicht.

Ohne ihn war nichts zu machen,
Keine Stunde hatt' er frei.
Gestern, als sie ihn begruben,
War er richtig auch dabei.

Selig sind die Auserwählten,
Die sich liebten und vermählten;
Denn sie tragen hübsche Früchte.
Und so wuchert die Geschichte
Sichtbarlich von Ort zu Ort.

The length and breadth of every land,
By every tree or shrub,
The ineffective human hand
Would sprout a trusty club.

I value graceful falsehood more,
The courtesy that eases;
I know the score, you know the score,
And every contact pleases.

Walter Arndt

He was busy, he was needed!
You could see him everywhere.
Church affairs or civic functions:
He was active, he was there.

Turkey shoot and Christmas dances,
Little League and charity,
Choir practice, beauty contests,
Always in the center: He.

Nothing could be done without him,
He was always on the go.
Yesterday, when he was buried,
Yes, you guessed it: He did show.

Dieter P. Lotze

Blest are the initiated,
Who in wedded love were mated,
For the pretty fruits they're showing.
And thus history keeps growing
Visibly from place to place.

Doch die braven Junggesellen,
Jungfern ohne Ehestellen,
Welche ohne Leibeserben,
So als Blattgewächse sterben,
Pflanzen sich durch Knollen fort.

Selbstkritik

Die Selbstkritik hat viel für sich.
Gesetzt den Fall, ich tadle mich,
So hab ich erstens den Gewinn,
Daß ich so hübsch bescheiden bin;
Zum zweiten denken sich die Leut,
Der Mann ist lauter Redlichkeit;
Auch schnapp ich drittens diesen Bissen
Vorweg den andern Kritiküssen;
Und viertens hoff ich außerdem
Auf Widerspruch, der mir genehm.
So kommt es denn zuletzt heraus,
Daß ich ein ganz famoses Haus.

Die Kleinsten

Sag Atome, sage Stäubchen.
Sind sie auch unendlich klein,
Haben sie doch ihre Leibchen
Und die Neigung da zu sein.

Yet the bachelor's situation,
Maidens with no marriage station,
Who no offspring leave behind them,
So as leaf-plants death will find them,
Grow as planted bulbs apace.

John Fitzell

Self-Critique

Much may be said for self-critique.
Say I point out where I am weak,

And right away I earn the credit
For modesty at having said it.

Next, people note what is so true:
This man is honest through and through.

Thirdly, I snatch a tasty morsel
From critics by my first endorsal.

Fourth, I may hope the accusation
Will spur a welcome refutation.

The final verdict: all in all,
There's nothing wrong with me at all.

Walter Arndt

The Smallest Ones

Call them atoms or corpuscles,
Far too small for us to see,
They have bodies, they have muscles,
And the stubborn trend to be.

Haben sie auch keine Köpfchen,
Sind sie doch voll Eigensinn.
Trotzig spricht das Zwerggeschöpfchen:
Ich will sein so wie ich bin.

Suche nur sie zu bezwingen,
Stark und findig wie du bist.
Solch ein Ding hat seine Schwingen,
Seine Kraft und seine List.

Kannst du auch aus ihnen schmieden
Deine Rüstung als Despot,
Schließlich wirst du doch ermüden,
Und dann heißt es: Er ist tot.

Sie stritten sich beim Wein herum,
Was das nun wieder wäre;
Das mit dem Darwin wär gar zu dumm
Und wider die menschliche Ehre.

Sie tranken manchen Humpen aus,
Sie stolperten aus den Türen,
Sie grunzten vernehmlich und kamen zu Haus
Gekrochen auf allen vieren.

Sie hat nichts und du desgleichen;
Dennoch wollt ihr, wie ich sehe,
Zu dem Bund der heil'gen Ehe
Euch bereits die Hände reichen.

Kinder, seid ihr denn bei Sinnen?
Überlegt euch das Kapitel!
Ohne die gehör'gen Mittel
Soll man keinen Krieg beginnen.

True, they have no heads nor features,
Yet each one has its own mind.
Clearly state the tiny creatures:
I'll be I, no other kind.

You are strong and you are clever,
Can control them for a while,
But they fly from you forever,
Show their strength and show their guile.

They will furnish, as required,
Arms for you that others dread.
Finally you will grow tired,
And the word will be: He's dead.

Dieter P. Lotze

The argument was loud, the wine
Was getting to their heads: How can
This stupid Darwin draw a line
Relating beasts to god-like man?

They drank some more, made many a speech,
They stumbled out through the doors,
They grunted, and snorted, and tried to reach
Their homes as they crawled on all fours.

Dieter P. Lotze

Not a dime in your possession,
Yet you feel you cannot wait,
Eager for the married state,
Wedding bells and gay procession?

Have you really lost your mind?
Think it over! Hold your horses!
No one should, without resources,
Start a war of any kind.

Dieter P. Lotze

Es sitzt ein Vogel auf dem Leim,
Er flattert sehr und kann nicht heim.
Ein schwarzer Kater schleicht herzu,
Die Krallen scharf, die Augen gluh.
Am Baum hinauf und immer höher
Kommt er dem armen Vogel näher.

Der Vogel denkt: Weil das so ist
Und weil mich doch der Kater frißt,
So will ich keine Zeit verlieren,
Will noch ein wenig quinquilieren
Und lustig pfeifen wie zuvor.
Der Vogel, scheint mir, hat Humor.

Die erste alte Tante sprach:
Wir müssen nun auch dran denken,
Was wir zu ihrem Namenstag
Dem guten Sophiechen schenken.

Drauf sprach die zweite Tante kühn:
Ich schlage vor, wir entscheiden
Uns für ein Kleid in Erbsengrün,
Das mag Sophiechen nicht leiden.

Der dritten Tante war das recht:
Ja, sprach sie, mit gelben Ranken!
Ich weiss, sie ärgert sich nicht schlecht
Und muss sich auch noch bedanken.

Sahst du das wunderbare Bild von Brouwer?
Es zieht dich an, wie ein Magnet.
Du lächelst wohl, derweil ein Schreckensschauer
Durch deine Wirbelsäule geht.

A bird is trapped up in a tree
By lime, no struggling sets it free.
Then, adding further to its woe,
With claws like knives and eyes aglow,
There comes a cat, a mean black beast,
Climbs up to get the welcome feast.

The bird thinks: I can't get away
And soon I'll be the tomcat's prey;
So let me not waste any time,
I'll gaily sing and trill and chime
Quite as before. This bird, I'd say
A sense of humor does display.

Dieter P. Lotze

The first old aunt said: I suggest
That we decide—the date is near—
What birthday present would be best
For Sophie, our niece so dear.

The second aunt said in great haste:
Let's buy for her a pea green dress.
We all know darling Sophie's taste;
There is not much she'd care for less.

Green's good, the third one did agree,
With yellow dots! We'll have a ball:
She's sure to get quite mad, you see,
And yet she'll have to thank us all.

Dieter P. Lotze

Did you see Brouwer's fascinating picture?
    It draws you as a magnet might,
You smile, of course, and yet a horror-stricture
    Will take you by the backbone tight.

Ein kühler Dokter öffnet einem Manne
    Die Schwäre hinten im Genick;
Daneben steht ein Weib mit einer Kanne,
    Vertieft in dieses Mißgeschick.

Ja, alter Freund, wir haben unsre Schwäre
    Meist hinten. Und voll Seelenruh
Drückt sie ein andrer auf. Es rinnt die Zähre,
    Und fremde Leute sehen zu.

Sie war ein Blümlein hübsch und fein,
Hell aufgeblüht im Sonnenschein.
Er war ein junger Schmetterling,
Der selig an der Blume hing.
Oft kam ein Bienlein mit Gebrumm
Und nascht und säuselt da herum.
Oft kroch ein Käfer kribbelkrab
Am hübschen Blümlein auf und ab.
Ach Gott, wie das dem Schmetterling
So schmerzlich durch die Seele ging.
Doch was am meisten ihn entsetzt,
Das Allerschlimmste kam zuletzt.
Ein alter Esel fraß die ganze
Von ihm so heiß geliebte Pflanze.

A doctor carefully and coolly lances
    His patient's ulcer in the nape;
Beside him with her tankard, this entrances
    A woman standing there agape.

O yes, old friend, we mostly have our swelling
    Behind. Another presses pus
Right out with peace of mind. The tears are welling
    And utter strangers look at us.

John Fitzell

    She was a flower fair and fine,
    Blooming bright in warm sunshine.
    A youthful butterfly was he
    Who hung upon her blessedly.
    Oft came a bee with humming sound
    And nipped and bumble-buzzed around.
    Oft cribble-crabbled a beetle who
    Crept up and down the flower too.
    O God, that made the butterfly
    Breathe out a painful, soulful sigh.
    Yet most of all what shocked him so,
    The worst thing was the final blow.
    An aged jackass gulped down neatly
    The plant that he had loved so sweetly.

John Fitzell

Christian Morgenstern

Gruselett

Der Flügelflagel gaustert
durchs Wiruwaruwolz,
die rote Fingur plaustert
und grausig gutzt der Golz.

Christian Morgenstern

Poetry translated by Max Knight except where otherwise noted

Scariboo

The Winglewangle phlutters
through widowadowood,
the crimson Fingoor splutters
and scary screaks the Scrood.

Der Lattenzaun

Es war einmal ein Lattenzaun,
mit Zwischenraum, hindurchzuschaun.

Ein Architekt, der dieses sah,
stand eines Abends plötzlich da—

und nahm den Zwischenraum heraus
und baute draus ein großes Haus.

Der Zaun indessen stand ganz dumm,
mit Latten ohne was herum.

Ein Anblick gräßlich und gemein.
Drum zog ihn der Senat auch ein.

Der Architekt jedoch entfloh
nach Afri- od- Ameriko.

Das aesthetische Wiesel

Ein Wiesel
saß auf einem Kiesel
inmitten Bachgeriesel.

Wißt ihr
weshalb?

Das Mondkalb
verriet es mir
im Stillen:

Das raffinier-
te Tier
tat's um des Reimes willen.

The Picket Fence

One time there was a picket fence
with space to gaze from hence to thence.

An architect who saw this sight
approached it suddenly one night,

removed the spaces from the fence,
and built of them a residence.

The picket fence stood there dumbfounded
with pickets wholly unsurrounded,

a view so loathsome and obscene,
the Senate had to intervene.

The architect, however, flew
to Afri- or Americoo.

The Aesthetic Weasel

A weasel
perched on an easel
within a patch of teasel.

But why
and how?

The Moon Cow
whispered her reply
one time:

The sopheest-
icated beest
did it just for the rhyme.

Das Mondschaf

Das Mondschaf steht auf weiter Flur.
Es harrt und harrt der großen Schur.
    Das Mondschaf.

Das Mondschaf rupft sich einen Halm
und geht dann heim auf seine Alm.
    Das Mondschaf.

Das Mondschaf spricht zu sich im Traum:
"Ich bin des Weltalls dunkler Raum."
    Das Mondschaf.

Das Mondschaf liegt am Morgen tot.
Sein Leib ist weiß, die Sonn' ist rot.
    Das Mondschaf.

Die beiden Esel

Ein finstrer Esel sprach einmal
zu seinem ehlichen Gemahl:

"Ich bin so dumm, du bist so dumm,
wir wollen sterben gehen, kumm!"

Doch wie es kommt so öfter eben:
Die beiden blieben fröhlich leben.

Das Geierlamm

Der Lämmergeier ist bekannt,
das Geierlamm erst hier genannt.

Der Geier, der ist offenkundig,
das Lamm hingegen untergrundig.

The Moonsheep

The moonsheep stands upon the clearing.
It waits and waits to get his shearing.
  The moonsheep.

The moonsheep plucks himself a blade
returning to his alpine glade.
  The moonsheep.

The moonsheep murmurs in his dream:
"I am the cosmos' gloomy scheme."
  The moonsheep.

The moonsheep, in the morn, lies dead.
His flesh is white, the sun is red.
  The moonsheep.

The Two Donkeys

A gloomy donkey, tir'd of life
one day addressed his wedded wife:

"I am so dumb, you are so dumb,
let's go and die together, come!"

But as befalls, time and again,
they lived on happily, the twain.

The Hawken Chick

The Chicken Hawk is widely known;
The Hawken Chick is all my own.

The Hawk swoops down rapaciously;
the Chick does things more graciously.

Es sagt nicht hu, es sagt nicht mäh
und frißt dich auf aus nächster Näh.

Und dreht das Auge dann zum Herrn.
Und alle haben's herzlich gern.

Der Leu

Auf einem Wandkalenderblatt
ein Leu sich abgebildet hat.

Er blickt dich an, bewegt und still,
den ganzen 17. April.

Wodurch er zu erinnern liebt,
daß es ihn immerhin noch gibt.

Die Schildkrökröte

"Ich bin nun tausend Jahre alt
und werde täglich älter;
der Gotenkönig Theobald
erzog mich im Behälter.

Seitdem ist mancherlei geschehn,
doch weiß ich nichts davon;
zur Zeit, da läßt für Geld mich sehn
ein Kaufmann zu Heilbronn.

Ich kenne nicht des Todes Bild
und nicht des Sterbens Nöte:
Ich bin die Schild- ich bin die Schild-
Ich bin die Schild-krö-kröte."

It does not cluck, it does not coo;
but when you're close, it swallows you,

then stands so innocent and mute
that all are saying: "My, how cute!"

Karl F. Ross

The Lion

A leaf of a calendar on the wall
displays a lion, grand and tall.

He views you regal and serene
the whole of April seventeen.

Reminding you, lest you forget,
that he is not extinct as yet.

The Tortoitoise

"I am a thousand seasons old
and getting on in age;
the Gothic ruler Theobold
confined me in a cage.

A lot has happened since that day,
but what, I do not know.
At present I am on display,
for money, in a show.

All talk of death I can ignore
as so much empty noise.
I am the tor-, I am the tor-,
I am the tor-toi-toise."

Möwenlied

Die Möwen sehen alle aus,
als ob sie Emma hießen.
Sie tragen einen weißen Flaus
und sind mit Schrot zu schießen.

Ich schieße keine Möwe tot,
ich laß sie lieber leben—
und füttre sie mit Roggenbrot
und rötlichen Zibeben.

O Mensch, du wirst nie nebenbei
der Möwe Flug erreichen.
Wofern du Emma heißest, sei
zufrieden, ihr zu gleichen.

Das Knie

Ein Knie geht einsam durch die Welt.
Es ist ein Knie, sonst nichts!
Es ist kein Baum! Es ist kein Zelt!
Es ist ein Knie, sonst nichts.

Im Kriege ward einmal ein Mann
erschossen um und um.
Das Knie allein blieb unverletzt—
als wär's ein Heiligtum.

Seitdem geht's einsam durch die Welt.
Es ist ein Knie, sonst nichts.
Es ist kein Baum, es ist kein Zelt.
Es ist ein Knie, sonst nichts.

The Seagulls

The seagulls by their looks suggest
that Emma is their name;
they wear a white and fluffy vest
and are the hunter's game.

I never shoot a seagull dead;
their life I do not take.
I like to feed them gingerbread
and bits of raisin cake.

O human, you will never fly
the way the seagulls do;
but if your name is Emma, why,
be glad they look like you.

Karl F. Ross

The Knee

On earth there roams a lonely knee.
It's just a knee, that's all.
It's not a tent, it's not a tree,
it's just a knee, that's all.

In battle, long ago, a man
was riddled through and through.
The knee alone escaped unhurt
as if it were taboo.

Since then there roams a lonely knee,
it's just a knee, that's all.
It's not a tent, it's not a tree,
it's just a knee, that's all.

Das Nasobēm

Auf seinen Nasen schreitet
einher das Nasobēm,
von seinem Kind begleitet.
Es steht noch nicht im Brehm.

Es steht noch nicht im Meyer.
Und auch im Brockhaus nicht.
Es trat aus meiner Leier
zum ersten Mal ans Licht.

Auf seinen Nasen schreitet
(wie schon gesagt) seitdem,
von seinem Kind begleitet,
einher das Nasobēm.

Bundeslied der Galgenbrüder

O schauerliche Lebenswirrn,
wir hängen hier am roten Zwirn!
Die Unke unkt, die Spinne spinnt,
und schiefe Scheitel kämmt der Wind.

O Greule, Greule, wüste Greule!
Du bist verflucht! so sagt die Eule.
Der Sterne Licht am Mond zerbricht.
Doch dich zerbrach's noch immer nicht.

O Greule, Greule, wüste Greule!
Hört ihr den Huf der Silbergäule?
Es schreit der Kauz: pardauz! pardauz!
da taut's, da graut's, da braut's, da blaut's!

The Nosobame

Upon his noses stalketh
around—the Nosobame;
with him, his offspring walketh.
He is not yet in Brehm,

you find him not in Meyer
nor does him Brockhaus cite.
He stepped forth from my lyre
the first time into light.

Upon his noses stalketh
—I will again proclaim—
(with him his offspring walketh),
since then, the Nosobame.

Chorus of the Gallows Gang

O life of horror-stricken dread!
We dangle from the crimson thread.
The spider spins, the croaker croaks,
and crookèd curls the nightwind strokes.

O growl, O growl, O rumbling growl!
Damned are your spirits, quoth the owl.
The starlight pales before the moon.
Will you yourself be paling soon?

O growl, O growl, O rumbling growl!
You hear the silver horses prowl?
The hooter hoots his weird hoo-hoos.
It dawns and dews and brews and blues.

Der Mond

Als Gott den lieben Mond erschuf,
gab er ihm folgenden Beruf:

Beim Zu- sowohl wie beim Abnehmen
sich deutschen Lesern zu bequemen,

ein $\mathcal{a}$ formierend und ein $\mathcal{Z}$ —
daß keiner groß zu denken hätt'.

Befolgend dies ward der Trabant
ein völlig deutscher Gegenstand.

Anto-logie

Im Anfang lebte, wie bekannt,
als größter Säuger der Gig-ant.

Wobei gig eine Zahl ist, die
es nicht mehr gibt,—so groß war sie!

Doch jene Größe schwand wie Rauch.
Zeit gab's genug—und Zahlen auch.

The Moon

When God had made the moon on high,
He did as follows specify:

while waning, waxing overhead,
her phase in German should be read,

an *α* describing and a *℥*
(read "Ab" and "Zu" in Germany).

And thus became what shines at night
a purely German satellite.

Anto-logy

Of yore, on earth was dominant
the biggest mammal: the Gig-ant.

("Gig" is a numeral so vast,
it's been extinct for ages past.)

But off, like smoke, that vastness flew.
Time did abound, and numbers too,

Bis eines Tags, ein winzig Ding,
der Zwölef-ant das Reich empfing.

Wo blieb sein Reich? Wo blieb er selb?—
Sein Bein wird im Museum gelb.

Zwar gab die gütige Natur
den Elef-anten uns dafur.

Doch ach, der Pulverpavian,
der Mensch voll Gier nach seinem Zahn,

erschießt ihn, statt ihm Zeit zu lassen,
zum Zehen-anten zu verblassen.

O "Klub zum Schutz der wilden Tiere",
hilf, daß der Mensch nicht ruiniere

die Sprossen dieser Riesenleiter,
die stets noch weiter führt und weiter!

Wie dankbar wird der Ant dir sein,
lässt du ihn wachsen und gedeihn,—

bis er dereinst im Nebel hinten
als Nulel-ant wird stumm verschwinden.

Der Zwölf-Elf

Der Zwölf-Elf hebt die linke Hand:
Da schlägt es Mitternacht im Land.

Es lauscht der Teich mit offnem Mund.
Ganz leise heult der Schluchtenhund.

Die Dommel reckt sich auf im Rohr.
Der Moorfrosch lugt aus seinem Moor.

until one day a tiny thing,
the Tweleph-ant, was chosen king.

Where is he now? Where is his throne?
In the museum pales his bone.

True, Mother Nature gave with grace
the Eleph-ant us in his place,

but, woe, that shooting anthropoid
called "Man," in quest for tusks destroyed

him ere he could degenerate,
by stages, to a Ten-ant's state.

O noble club, SPCA,
don't let Man wholly take away

the steps of that titanic scale
that leads still farther down the trail.

How grateful will the Ant survive
if left to flourish and to thrive,

until he, in a far-off year,
as Zero-ant will disappear.

The Twelve Nix

The Twelve Nix raises up his hand
and midnight strikes throughout the land.

The gaping pond in silence harks;
the canyon canine softly barks.

The bittern rises from its bog;
out of his swampland peers the frog.

Der Schneck horcht auf in seinem Haus;
desgleichen die Kartoffelmaus.

Das Irrlicht selbst macht Halt und Rast
auf einem windgebrochnen Ast.

Sophie, die Maid, hat ein Gesicht:
Das Mondschaf geht zum Hochgericht.

Die Galgenbrüder wehn im Wind.
Im fernen Dorfe schreit ein Kind.

Zwei Maulwürf küssen sich zur Stund
als Neuvermählte auf den Mund.

Hingegen tief im finstern Wald
ein Nachtmahr seine Fäuste ballt:

Dieweil ein später Wanderstrumpf
sich nicht verlief in Teich und Sumpf.

Der Rabe Ralf ruft schaurig: "Kra!
Das End ist da! Das End ist da!"

Der Zwölf-Elf senkt die linke Hand:
Und wieder schläft das ganze Land.

Ukas

Durch Anschlag mach ich euch bekannt:
Heut ist kein Fest im deutschen Land.
Drum sei der Tag für alle Zeit
zum Nichtfest-Feiertag geweiht.

The snail perks up within his house,
and likewise the potato mouse.

The will o' wisp has stopped its jig
and rests upon a broken twig.

Sophia dreams, the hangman's wench:
The moonsheep pleads before the bench.

The gallows gang sways up and down;
an infant cries far off in town.

Two moles, just married, turn about
and kiss each other on the snout.

While deep within the forest's mist
an angry nightmare shakes his fist

because a hiker, late on tour,
did not get lost in pond and moor.

The Raven Ralph calls out in fear:
"The end is near, the end is near!"

The Twelve Nix, now, puts down his hand
and sleep again enshrouds the land.

Karl F. Ross

Ukase

I made it known by proclamation:
Today's no feast day in this nation.
Wherefore this day forever may
be fêted as Nonholiday.

Das Gebet

Die Rehlein beten zur Nacht,
hab acht!

Halb neun!

Halb zehn!

Halb elf!

Halb zwölf!

Zwölf!

Die Rehlein beten zur Nacht,
hab acht!
Sie falten die kleinen Zehlein,
die Rehlein.

Fisches Nachtgesang

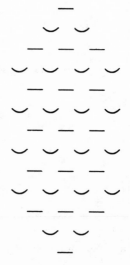

The Does' Prayer

The does, as the hour grows late,
med-it-ate;

med-it-nine;

med-i-ten;

med-eleven;

med-twelve;

mednight!

The does, as the hour grows late,
meditate.
They fold their little toesies,
the doesies.

Fish's Night Song

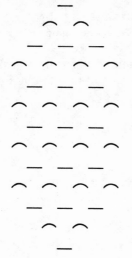

Die Trichter

Zwei Trichter wandeln durch die Nacht.
Durch ihres Rumpfs verengten Schacht
fließt weißes Mondlicht
still und heiter
auf ihren
Waldweg
u. s.
w.

Der Schnupfen

Ein Schnupfen hockt auf der Terrasse,
auf daß er sich ein Opfer fasse

—und stürzt alsbald mit großem Grimm
auf einen Menschen namens Schrimm.

Paul Schrimm erwidert prompt: Pitschü!
und *hat* ihn drauf bis Montag früh.

Vice Versa

Ein Hase sitzt auf einer Wiese,
des Glaubens, niemand sähe diese.

Doch, im Besitze eines Zeißes,
betrachtet voll gehaltnen Fleißes

The Funnels

A funnel ambles through the night.
Within its body, moonbeams white
    converge as they
      descend upon
        its forest
        pathway
        and
         so
         on
         .

Karl F. Ross

The Sniffle

A sniffle crouches on the terrace
to catch a victim he could harass.

And suddenly he jumps with vim
upon a man by name of Schrimm.

Paul Schrimm, responding with "hatchoo,"
is stuck with him the weekend through.

Vice Versa

A rabbit sits upon the green
believing it can not be seen.

A man, though, with a telescope
and watching keenly on a slope

vom vis-à-vis gelegnen Berg
ein Mensch den kleinen Löffelzwerg.

Ihn aber blickt hinwiederum
ein Gott von fern an, mild und stumm.

Golch und Flubis

Golch und Flubis, das sind zwei
Gaukler aus der Titanei,

die mir einst in einer Nacht
Zri, die große Zra vermacht.

Mangelt irgend mir ein Ding,
Ein Beweis, ein Baum, ein Ring—

ruf ich Golch und er verwandelt
sich in das, worum sich's handelt.

Während Flubis umgekehrt
das wird, was man gern entbehrt.

Bei z.B. Halsbeschwerden
wird das Halsweh Flubis werden.

Fällte dich z.B. Mord,
ging' der Tod als Flubis fort.

Lieblich lebt es sich mit solchen
wackern Flubissen und Golchen.

Darum suche jeder ja
dito Zri, die große Zra.

extending from a near-by knoll,
observes the little spoon-eared troll.

The man, in turn, from far is seen
by God, reposeful and serene.

Golch and Flubis

Golch and Flubis, these are two
sorcerers from Shangri-loo

who, one night, were given me
by the mighty Zra queen, Zri.

If I lack a certain thing,
—say, a proof, a tree, a ring—

I call Golch, who will with speed
change himself to what I need.

Flubis, contrary to this,
turns to what one wants to miss.

If a painful throat your plight is,
Flubis flees as laryngitis.

If a slayer stabbed your heart,
Flubis would as Death depart.

Life's a lark, indeed, when these
Golches help and Flubises.

Fortunate, therefore, is he
who wins grace from Zra queen Zri.

Himmel und Erde

Der Nachtwindhund weint wie ein Kind,
dieweil sein Fell von Regen rinnt.

Jetzt jagt er wild das Neumondweib,
das hinflieht mit gebognem Leib.

Tief unten geht, ein dunkler Punkt,
querüberfeld ein Forstadjunkt.

Das Lied vom blonden Korken

Ein blonder Korke spiegelt sich
in einem Lacktablett—
allein er säh' sich dennoch nich,
selbst wenn er Augen hätt'!

Das macht, dieweil er senkrecht steigt
zu seinem Spiegelbild!
Wenn man ihn freilich seitwärts neigt,
zerfällt, was oben gilt.

O Mensch, gesetzt, du spiegelst dich
im, sagen wir,—im All!
Und senkrecht!—wärest du dann nich
ganz in demselben Fall?

Der Traum der Magd

Am Morgen spricht die Magd ganz wild:
Ich hab heut nacht ein Kind gestillt—

ein Kind mit einem Käs als Kopf—
und einem Horn am Hinterschopf!

Heaven and Earth

The nightwindhound wails like a child,
his rain-soaked hide is all defiled.

He's hunting now the newmoondame
who flees along with twisted frame.

Way down below a darkish dot
—the ranger—walks across the lot.

The Song of the Yellow Cork

A golden cork is, mirror-wise,
shown by a polished shelf;
yet, even if endowed with eyes,
it could not see itself.

This is because it stands aligned
with its reflected view;
but if it sideways is inclined,
such is no longer true.

O man, suppose you did reflect
straight up, let's say, in space:
Would this not have the same effect
as in the stated case!

The Maid's Dream

When morning came, the maid went wild
and raved: "Last night I nursed a child—

"a child who wore a cheese as head,
and from its hair a horn outspread.

Das Horn, o denkt euch, war aus Salz
und ging zu essen, und dann—

                             "Halt's—
halt's Maul!" so spricht die Frau, "und geh
an deinen Dienst, Zä-zi-li-ē!"

Korf erfindet eine Art von Witzen . . .

Korf erfindet eine Art von Witzen,
die erst viele Stunden später wirken.
Jeder hört sie an mit langer Weile.

Doch, als hätt' ein Zunder still geglommen,
wird man nachts im Bette plötzlich munter,
selig lächelnd wie ein satter Säugling.

Die Korfsche Uhr

Korf erfindet eine Uhr,
die mit zwei Paar Zeigern kreist,
und damit nach vorn nicht nur,
sondern auch nach rückwärts weist.

Zeigt sie zwei,—somit auch zehn;
zeigt sie drei,—somit auch neun;
und man braucht nur hinzusehn,
um die Zeit nicht mehr zu scheun.

Denn auf dieser Uhr von Korfen,
mit dem janushaften Lauf,
(dazu ward sie so entworfen):
hebt die Zeit sich selber auf.

"The horn—just think!—was salty, but
was fit to eat, and after . . ."

                            "Shut—
shut up," the mistress said, "and see
about your duties, Ce-ci-lee!"

Korf's Joke

Korf invents a novel kind of joke
which won't take effect for many hours.
Everyone is bored when first he hears it.

But he will, as though a fuse were burning,
suddenly wake up in bed at night time,
smiling sweetly like a well-fed baby.

Korf's Clock

Korf a kind of clock invents
where two pairs of hands go round:
one the current hour presents,
one is always backward bound.

When it's two—it's also ten;
when it's three—it's also nine.
You just look at it, and then
time gets never out of line.

for in Korf's astute invention
with its Janus-kindred stride
(which, of course, was his intention)
time itself is nullified.

Palmströms Uhr

Palmströms Uhr ist andrer Art,
reagiert mimosisch zart.

Wer sie bittet, wird empfangen.
Oft schon ist sie so gegangen,

wie man herzlich sie gebeten,
ist zurück- und vorgetreten,

eine Stunde, zwei, drei Stunden,
je nachdem sie mitempfunden.

Selbst als Uhr, mit ihren Zeiten,
will sie nicht Prinzipien reiten:

Zwar ein Werk, wie allerwärts,
doch zugleich ein Werk—mit Herz.

Palmström

Palmstöm steht an einem Teiche
und entfaltet groß ein rotes Taschentuch:
Auf dem Tuch ist eine Eiche
dargestellt, sowie ein Mensch mit einem Buch.

Palmström wagt nicht, sich hineinzuschneuzen.
Er gehört zu jenen Käuzen,
die oft unvermittelt-nackt
Ehrfurcht vor dem Schönen packt.

Zärtlich faltet er zusammen,
was er eben erst entbreitet.
Und kein Fühlender wird ihn verdammen,
weil er ungeschneuzt entschreitet.

Palmstroem's Clock

Palmstroem's clock—a different kind—
is mimosa-like designed.

All requests are kindly heeded:
Many times the clock proceeded

at the pace that folks were urging
—slowing up or forward surging

for one hour, or two, or three,
as impelled by sympathy.

Though a timepiece, it will never
stick to petty rules, however.

Just a clockwork, slick and smart,
yet a clockwork with a heart.

Palmstroem

Palmstroem stands beside a pond
where a scarlet handkerchief he wide unfolds;
on it shows an oak tree and, beyond,
a lone person and a book he holds.

Palmstroem does not dare to blow his nose;
he is plainly one of those
who at times, with sudden start,
feel a reverence for art.

He refolds with tender skill
what he just had spread out clean,
and no gentle soul will wish him ill
if, with nose unblown, he leaves the scene.

Karl F. Ross and Max Knight

Die unmögliche Tatsache

Palmström, etwas schon an Jahren,
wird an einer Strasenbeuge
und von einem Kraftfahrzeuge
überfahren.

"Wie war" (spricht er, sich erhebend
und entschlossen weiterlebend)
"möglich, wie dies Unglück, ja—:
daß es überhaupt geschah?

"Ist die Staatskunst anzuklagen
in Bezug auf Kraftfahrwagen?
Gab die Polizeivorschrift
hier dem Fahrer freie Trift?

"Oder war vielmehr verboten,
hier Lebendige zu Toten
umzuwandeln,—kurz und schlicht:
Durfte hier der Kutscher nicht—?"

Eingehüllt in feuchte Tücher,
prüft er die Gesetzesbücher
und ist alsobald im Klaren:
Wagen durften dort nicht fahren!

Und er kommt zu dem Ergebnis:
Nur ein Traum war das Erlebnis.
Weil, so schliesst er messerscharf,
nicht sein *kann*, was nicht sein *darf*.

Geburtsakt der Philosophie

Erschrocken staunt der Heide Schaf mich an,
als säh's in mir den ersten Menschenmann.
Sein Blick steckt an; wir stehen wie im Schlaf;
mir ist, ich säh zum ersten Mal ein Schaf.

The Impossible Fact

Palmstroem, old, an aimless rover,
walking in the wrong direction
at a busy intersection
is run over.

"How, now," he announces rising
and with firmness death despising,
"can an accident like this
ever happen? What's amiss?

"Did the state administration
fail in motor transportation?
Under the police chief's sway
had the driver right of way?

"Isn't there a prohibition,
barring motorized transmission
of the living to the dead?
Did the driver lose his head?"

Tightly swathed in dampened tissues
he explores the legal issues,
and it soon is clear as air:
Cars were not permitted there!

And he comes to the conclusion:
His mishap was an illusion,
for, he reasons pointedly,
that which *must* not, *can* not be.

Birth of Philosophy

The heath sheep glares at me with frightened awe
as though I were the first of men it saw.
Contagious glare! We stand as though asleep;
it seems the first time that I see a sheep.

Der Werwolf

Ein Werwolf eines Nachts entwich
von Weib und Kind, und sich begab
an eines Dorfschullehrers Grab
und bat ihn: Bitte, beuge mich!

Der Dorfschulmeister stieg hinauf
auf seines Blechschilds Messingknauf
und sprach zum Wolf, der seine Pfoten
geduldig kreuzte vor dem Toten:

"Der Werwolf,—sprach der gute Mann,
"des Weswolfs, Genetiv sodann,
"dem Wemwolf, Dativ, wie man's nennt,
"den Wenwolf,—damit hat's ein End'."

Dem Werwolf schmeichelten die Fälle,
er rollte seine Augenälle.
Indessen, bat er, füge doch
zur Einzahl auch die Mehrzahl noch!

Der Dorfschulmeister aber mußte
gestehn, dass er von ihr nichts wußte.
Zwar Wölfe gäb's in großer Schar,
doch 'Wer' gäb's nur im Singular.

Der Wolf erhob sich tränenblind—
er hatte ja doch Weib und Kind!!
Doch da er kein Gelehrter eben,
so schied er dankend und ergeben.

The Banshee

[An Analogy]

One night, a banshee slunk away
from mate and child, and in the gloom
went to a village teacher's tomb,
requesting him: "Inflect me, pray."

The village teacher climbed up straight
upon his grave stone with its plate
and to the apparition said
who meekly knelt before the dead:

"The banSHEE, in the subject's place;
the banHERS, the possessive case.
The banHER, next, is what they call
objective case—and that is all."

The banshee marveled at the cases
and writhed with pleasure, making faces,
but said: "You did not add, so far,
the plural to the singular!"

The teacher, though, admitted then
that this was not within his ken.
"While 'bans' are frequent," he advised,
"a 'she' cannot be pluralized."

The banshee, rising clammily,
wailed: "What about my family?"
Then, being not a learned creature,
said humbly "Thanks" and left the teacher.

Karl F. Ross

Die Probe

Zu einem seltsamen Versuch
erstand ich mir ein Nadelbuch.

Und zu dem Buch ein altes zwar,
doch äußerst kühnes Dromedar.

Ein Reicher auch daneben stand,
zween Säcke Gold in jeder Hand.

Der Reiche ging alsdann herfür
und klopfte an die Himmelstür.

Drauf Petrus sprach: "Geschrieben steht,
das ein Kamel weit eher geht

durchs Nadelöhr als du, du Heid,
durch diese Türe groß und breit!"

Ich, glaubend fest an Gottes Wort,
ermunterte das Tier sofort,

ihm zeigend hinterm Nadelöhr
ein Zuckerhörnchen als Douceur.

Und in der Tat! Das Vieh ging durch,
obzwar sich quetschend wie ein Lurch!

Der Reiche aber sah ganz stier
und sagte nichts als: "Wehe mir!"

The Test

To set up an experiment
some money I on needles spent

and on a camel which, though old,
was quite exceptionally bold.

Near me a rich man took his stand,
twain bags of gold in either hand.

The rich man did not hesitate
to knock upon the pearly gate.

St. Peter answered: "It is writ:
A needle's eye will ere permit

a camel's body to pass through
than this wide gate make way for you."

I, trusting fully God's command,
at once cajoled the creature and

displayed behind the needle's eye
a tempting piece of sugar pie.

And so indeed! Through went the brute,
although it wiggled like a newt.

The rich man, though, stared gloomily
and said no word but: "Woe is me!"

Bim, Bam, Bum

Ein Glockenton fliegt durch die Nacht,
als hätt' er Vogelflügel;
er fliegt in römischer Kirchentracht
wohl über Tal und Hügel.

Er sucht die Glockentönin BIM,
die ihm vorausgeflogen;
d.h. die Sache ist sehr schlimm,
sie hat ihn nämlich betrogen.

"O komm" so ruft er, "komm, dein BAM
erwartet dich voll Schmerzen.
Komm wieder, BIM, geliebtes Lamm,
dein BAM liebt dich von Herzen!"

Doch BIM, daß ihr's nur alle wißt,
hat sich dem BUM ergeben;
der ist zwar auch ein guter Christ,
allein das ist es eben.

Der BAM fliegt weiter durch die Nacht
wohl über Wald und Lichtung.
Doch, ach, er fliegt umsonst! Das macht,
er fliegt in falscher Richtung.

Der Sperling und das Känguru

In seinem Zaun das Känguru—
es hockt und guckt dem Sperling zu.

Der Sperling sitzt auf dem Gebäude—
doch ohne sonderliche Freude.

Vielmehr, er fühlt, den Kopf geduckt,
wie ihn das Känguru beguckt.

Ding Dong Dang

A bell sound flies through night in search,
as if on bird wings soaring;
he flies in the garb of the Roman Church,
the hills and dales exploring.

He seeks the lady bell sound DING
who'd winged away before him;
they have to settle a serious thing:
she broke the troth she swore him.

"O come," he calls, "O come. Your DONG
awaits you, pet, with anguish.
Return, my DING, for whom I long,
don't let your sweetheart languish!"

But DING had yielded, it is true,
to DANG's gallant devices;
he is an honest Christian too—
that's just what caused the crisis.

So DONG continues through the night
through bare and wooded section.
He flies, alas, in vain: His flight
is in the wrong direction.

The Sparrow and the Kangaroo

Behind the fence, the kangaroo
has on a sparrow cast his view.

The sparrow perches on the pale—
he doesn't feel too hap and hale.

Uneasily he feels, instead,
the mammal's gaze and ducks his head.

Der Sperling sträubt den Federflaus—
die Sache ist auch gar zu kraus.

Ihm ist, als ob er kaum noch säße . . .
Wenn nun das Känguru ihn fräße?!

Doch dieses dreht nach einer Stunde
den Kopf, aus irgend einem Grunde,

vielleicht auch ohne tiefern Sinn,
nach einer andern Richtung hin.

Der Rabe Ralf

Der Rabe Ralf
    will will hu hu
dem niemand half
    still still du du
half sich allein
am Rabenstein
    will will still still
      hu hu

Die Nebelfrau
    will will hu hu
nimmt's nicht genau
    still still du du
sie sagt nimm nimm
's ist nicht so schlimm
    will will still still
      hu hu

The sparrow ruffles up his wings—
he doesn't trust the looks of things.

A terror threatens to unseat him:
What if the kangaroo should eat him?

The latter, though, will briefly pause,
then turn his head, perhaps for cause

(or possibly without reflection)
unto a different direction.

The Raven Ralph

[Who Ate Gallows Food]

The Raven Ralph
    will will hoo hoo,
he halped himsalf
    still still do do
all on his own
at Raven's Stone
    will will still still
        hoo hoo.

The Maid of Mist
    will will hoo hoo
knows every twist
    still still do do
"Take, take," said she,
" 'tis all for free."
    Will will still still
        hoo hoo.

Doch als ein Jahr
will will hu hu
vergangen war
still still du du
da lag im Rot
der Rabe tot
will will still still
du du

Der Nachtschelm und das Siebenschwein
ODER **Eine glückliche Ehe**

Der Nachtschelm und das Siebenschwein,
die gingen eine Ehe ein,
o wehe!
Sie hatten dreizehn Kinder, und
davon war eins der Schluchtenhund,
zwei andre waren Rehe.

Das vierte war die Rabenmaus,
das fünfte war ein Schneck samt Haus,
o Wunder!
Das sechste war ein Käuzelein,
das siebte war ein Siebenschwein
und lebte in Burgunder.

Acht war ein Gürteltier nebst Gurt,
neun starb sofort nach der Geburt,
o wehe!
Von zehn bis dreizehn ist nicht klar;
doch wie dem auch gewesen war,
es war eine glückliche Ehe!

But when at last
    will will hoo hoo
a year had passed
    still still do do
the sun rose red,
and Ralph lay dead
    will will still still
        do do.

Karl F. Ross

The Nightrogue and the Sevenswine
OR A Happy Pair

The Nightrogue and the Sevenswine
in matrimony did combine,
    beware!
Soon thirteen offspring came around;
the first one was the canyonhound
and two were doesies fair.

The fourth one was the ravenmouse,
the fifth one was a snail with house,
    what sport!
A hooting owl was sixth in line,
the seventh was a sevenswine
who lived in purple port.

Eighth came an earth hog, down to earth;
the ninth died shortly after birth,
    beware!
Whatever may the fate have been
of ten, eleven, twelve, thirteen—
there was a happy pair!

Der Gingganz

Ein Stiefel wandern und sein Knecht
von Knickebühl gen Entenbrecht.

Urplötzlich auf dem Felde drauß
begehrt der Stiefel: Zieh mich aus!

Der Knecht drauf: Es ist nicht an dem;
doch sagt mir, lieber Herre,—!: wem?

Dem Stiefel gibt es einen Ruck:
Fürwahr, beim heiligen Nepomuk,

ich GING GANZ in Gedanken hin . . .
Du weißt, dass ich ein andrer bin,

seitdem ich meinen Herrn verlor . . .
Der Knecht wirft beide Arm' empor,

als wollt er sagen: Laß doch, laß!
Und weiter zieht das Paar fürbaß.

Der Glaube

Eines Tags bei Kohlhaasficht
sah man etwas Wunderbares.
Doch daß zweifellos und wahr es,
dafür bürgt das Augenlicht.

Nämlich standen dort zwei Hügel,
höchst solid und wohl bestellt;
einen schmückten Windmühlflügel
und den andern ein Kornfeld.

The Wentall

A boot was walking with his jack
from Haverstraw to Hackensack.

Then, suddenly, among the trees,
the boot demanded: "Strip me, please!"

The jack replied: "Yes, Sir, why not;
but, may I ask—of whom or what?"

The boot, at that, was thunderstruck
and answered: "Holy Nepomuk!

I WENT ALL lost in thought, bemused—
you know, I have been quite confused

since I have lost my master, so . . ."
The jack threw up his arms as though

he meant to say: "Why should I care?"
And further trudged along the pair.

Faith

One fine day near Abecee
lo! a myst'ry came about.
It was true without a doubt,
as was plain for all to see.

There two hills were situated,
solid, stable, not to yield—
one was windmill-decorated,
one embellished by a field.

Plötzlich eines Tags um viere
wechselten die Plätze sie;
furchtbar brüllten die Dorfstiere,
und der Mensch fiel auf das Knie.

Doch der Bauer Anton Metzer,
weit berühmt als frommer Mann,
sprach: ich war der Landumsetzer,
zeigt mich nur dem Landrat an.

Niemand anders als mein Glaube
hat die Berge hier versetzt.
Daß sich keiner was erlaube:
Denn ich fühle stark mich jetzt.

Aller Auge stand gigantisch
offen, als er dies erzählt.
Doch das Land war protestantisch
und in Dalldorf starb ein Held.

On that day, then, close to seven,
both changed places suddenly;
ghastly roared the bulls to heaven,
every man dropped on his knee.

But Al Metzer, local granger,
well-known pious man of peace,
said: "*I* was the landscape changer.
Go, complain to the police!

Nothing but my firm conviction
and my faith moved mountains here.
I heed no one's contradiction,
I feel strong, let this be clear!"

But this magical solution
the agnostic state denied;
sent him to an institution,
where the man, a martyr, died.

Kurt Tucholsky

Essay on Man

Man has two legs and two sets of convictions: one for good times and one for bad ones. The latter is called Religion.

Man is a vertebrate animal and has an immortal soul, as well as a fatherland, just so he won't get too cocky.

Man is produced in a natural way, but he considers it unnatural and doesn't like to talk about it. He is made, but he isn't asked whether he wants to be.

Man is a useful creature, because he serves to make oil stocks rise through war casualties, to increase mine owners' profits through mining casualties, as well as serving culture, art, and science.

Besides the urges to procreate and to eat and drink, man has two passions: to make a row and not to listen. One could just about define man as a creature that never listens. A wise man does well not to listen, because he seldom gets to hear anything sensible. What men like to hear is promises, flattery, appreciation, and compliments. When flattering, it is advisable that one pile it on three grades thicker than one would think possible.

Man begrudges his kind everything, which is why he invented laws. He mustn't, so the others shouldn't either.

To rely on man, one does well to sit on him; then one is certain, at least for a while, that he won't run away. Some, to be sure, also rely on his character.

Man breaks down into two parts: a male part which doesn't want to think, and a female one which is unable to. Both have so-called emotions; the surest way to arouse them is to sensitize certain nerve spots of the organism. In such cases, some men secrete lyric poetry.

Man is a herbivorous and carnivorous creature. On North Pole expeditions he occasionally devours specimens of his own kind; but this is compensated for by Fascism.

Man is a political animal which likes best to spend its life massed into clumps. Each clump hates the other clumps because they are the others, and hates its own clump because it is its own. This latter hatred is called Patriotism.

Every man has a liver, a spleen, a pair of lungs, and a flag; all four organs are vital. There are said to be men without a liver or a spleen and with only one lung; there are no men without a flag.

Man likes to stimulate weak procreative activity, and for this he has various resources: bullfights, crime, sports, and jurisprudence.

Men conjointly do not exist. There are only men who master and others who are mastered. But no one has yet mastered himself, because the opposing slave is always mightier than the domineering master. Every man is his own inferior.

When man feels that he can no longer kick up his heels, he becomes pious and wise; then he gives up the sour grapes of the world. This is called contemplation. Man's various stages of life regard one another as different races; oldsters usually have forgotten that they were young once, or they forget that they are old, and young people never comprehend that they can grow old.

Man doesn't like to die because he doesn't know what happens afterward. If he imagines he does, he still doesn't like to die, because he wants to continue for a little while longer in the old way. For "a little while longer," read "forever."

For the rest, man is a creature that knocks, makes bad music, and lets his dog bark. Sometimes he leaves one in peace, but then he is dead.

Besides men there are Saxons and Americans, but we won't take them up until next year, when we have Zoology.

Harry Zohn

The Social Psychology of Holes

The most important things are done through tubes.
Proof: genitals, pens, and guns.

—Lichtenberg

A hole is where something isn't.

The hole is a permanent companion of the non-hole; I'm sorry, but there is no such thing as a hole by itself. If there were something everywhere, there would be no holes, but there wouldn't be any philosophy either, not to mention religion, which is holey in origin. A mouse couldn't exist without a hole, nor could man. It is the final salvation for both when they are hard-pressed by matter. A hole is always a Good Thing.

When a man hears the word "hole," he has associations; some think of touchhole, others of buttonhole, still others of Goebbels.

Holes are the foundation of our social order, and that about describes same. Workers live in a hole in the wall, they always find themselves in a hole, and if they get out of line they are thrown in the hole, although they need being holed-up like a hole in the head. Being born in their slums is a curse; but why did the children have to come out of that particular hole? A few holes farther, and the kids would have been assured of going to law school.

The strangest thing about a hole is its edge. It's still part of the Something, but it constantly overlooks the Nothing—a border guard of matter. Nothingness has no such guard; while the molecules at the edge of a hole get dizzy because they are staring into a hole, the molecules of the hole get . . . firmy? There's no word for it. For our language was created by the Something people; the Hole people speak a language of their own.

A hole is something static; there are no holes in transit. Well, hardly any.

Holes that get married become One—one of the strangest among the processes that cannot be imagined. If you knock down the dividing wall between two holes, does the right edge belong to the left hole? Or the left edge to the right hole? Or each to each? Or both to both? (I should have my worries!)

If a hole is plugged up, where does it go? Does it squeeze to the side and merge with matter? Or does it run to another hole to pour out its heart? What happens to the plugged-up hole? Nobody knows; there is a hole in our knowledge.

Where one thing is, there cannot be another. Where there already is one hole, can there be another?

And why are there no semi-holes?

Some objects are devalued by one little hole: because there is nothing in a single place, all the rest isn't worth anything. Examples: a railroad ticket, a virgin, a balloon.

The thing-in-itself* is still being searched for; a hole already is "in itself." Only someone with one foot in the hole and the other here among us would be truly wise; but they say that no one has managed to do this yet. Megalomaniacs claim that a hole is something negative. That is incorrect; a man is a non-hole, and the hole is the primary thing. Hole your horses! A hole is the only foretaste of paradise that we have down here. Only when you are dead will you know what living is.

Pardon this piece; I merely wanted to fill the hole between the previous selection and the next one.

Harry Zohn

Angler, Compleat with Piety

There's a man near Ascona, Switzerland, who's got religion and loves all living creatures, everything that crawls and flies. Well and good. But the man happens to like fishing. So he sometimes sits by Lake Maggiore, swinging his legs, holding his fishing rod and looking into the water. And as he does so he prays.

He prays that no fish should bite.

You see, the fish are being tortured when they squirm on the hook, and the man wouldn't want that. So he sends one fervent prayer after another to the Good Lord, Lake Maggiore Fish Division, to keep the fish from taking his bait. And then he goes on angling.

*Kant's concept of the "*Ding an sich.*"—H.Z.

My dear readers! Isn't this man a typical allegory, a symbol even? That's what he is. That man must be an old Jew, or—an extreme case of Jewishness—he must have had Jesuit training. He has attained the highest level that a man can reach. He has learned how to reconcile heavenly ideals with his sinful drives, and that requires real skill. It may not make any difference to the fish wriggling on his hook, but to him it does make a difference, for now he has both: the fish and peace of mind.

Conclusion and general application: There they sit by the banks of life—or by the sea of life, that's really much better—there they sit by the sea of life, swinging their legs and dangling their lines into the water in order to hook success. But if they're shrewd, they pray at the same time, which makes them: whores who've got religion; civic-minded bank directors; democratic militarists; and journalists who oh-so-privately love truth. They prey and they pray.

Harry Zohn

Someday Somebody Should . . .

Someday somebody should secretly note down in shorthand what people really say. No naturalism even comes close. To be sure: there are plays in which the authors take great pains to imitate real life—though always with the necessary "epic abridgement" (as Fontane called it, who found Raabe lacking in the same), always slightly stylized, tailored as it were to suit the needs of play or book. That won't do.

No, somebody should take it down word for word—at a hundred-eighty syllables a minute—precisely the way it's spoken. The results, I believe, would confirm the following:

Everyday language is a dense wood, a forest overgrown with the creeping vine of filler words and phrases. We need hardly mention the standard windup, "Know what I mean?" (pronounced: "no-wadameen?"). Nor that: "Matches, please!" is a sheer impossibility, an Everest of incivility. Of course, it really goes more like this: "Pardon me, would you be so kind, the matches please, if it's not too much trouble? Thank you. Don't mention it. Thank you!"—that's how it goes.

But let people start swapping stories—then the real fun begins. Language staggers like a chicken without a head, grammar gets run ragged—oh tempora! oh modi!

The first law of conversation: your partner is hard of hearing and a little feeble-minded—it is therefore advisable to say everything six times. "So he says to me, he says he can't give me the bill! Just like that, he says: he can't give me the bill! Well for heaven's sake—if I says to him politely, Mr. Wittkopp, will you please give me the bill, he can't just say, I can't give you the bill! But that's exactly what he said. Can you believe it? Just like that, he says . . ." and on and on.

A related practice is the instant echo that some people like to tag onto every punchline. "So then he looks at her real sadly and he says: You know—I'm an old man: I'd sooner have a glass o' beer and a good cigar instead!" Pause. "I'd sooner have a glass o' beer and a good cigar instead. Haha." It's like seltzer bubbling back up through the nose . . .

Second law: everyday language has a grammar all its own. In Berlin, for instance, they use a suspended future tense. "So I'm walkin' down 'a street, see—betcha dat goofball's gonna go: 'N doncha faget ta give da goyl da ring! So nachally I'm gonna take off my left galosh 'n clobber 'im . . .'"

Third law: a good everyday dialogue never ever runs like a theater dialogue: with statement followed by repartee. That's a literary fabrication. In your everyday dialogue there are only speakers—no listeners. The two strands of the conversation run right past each other, rubbing elbows at times, it's true—but on the whole it's every man for himself. Here's where that lovely transition, "No," comes in handy. For instance:

"I don't know (very important introductory expression)—I don't know: if I don't get to smoke my cigar after lunch, I can't work all day." (Careless logic: he means all afternoon.) To which the other responds: "No." (Completely idiotic. He doesn't mean "no" at all. What he means is: Me, I'm different. And besides . . .) "No. See, if I smoke after lunch, then . . ." and what follows is an exact blow by blow account of no interest to anyone.

Fourth law: That which must get said, must get said, even if nobody's listening, even if the moment has been missed, even if it's now totally out of place. What gets shouted around in your average "animated conversation"—nobody has ever noted it down. But somebody should someday. The way lousy punchlines and a few good ones too explode and vanish into thin air for the sole sake of the dear little angels above, the way not one link in the general mayhem hooks into another, but rather, as though with pincers extended, everybody keeps grabbing for something that isn't there: a lot of hats without heads, shoestrings without shoes, single twins . . . it's really rather remarkable.

Oh the unwritten language of everyday! If only somebody'd write it down someday! Just the way it's spoken: unabridged, unadorned, no makeup, no plastic surgery! Somebody should note it down.

And then the whole garble ought to be spoken onto a grammophone record and played back for the benefit of those who spoke it. They'd shudder then and run off to see a nice play, you know the kind, Fritz, take your feet off the table, where the actors speak so nice and naturally, just like in real life, you mean you really think Miss Bergner is, not me, I don't think she is at all, I mean, to me she's just too . . .

Somebody should note it down.

Peter Wortsman

The Creed of the Bourgeoisie

The bourgeoisie is not very edifying in any country. National characteristics can tone down specific qualities or accentuate them; it seems that precisely this range of income and property determines a mentality that makes people shallow and hardened, chauvinistic out of anxiety, heartless out of narrowness of horizon, and rude out of lack of imagination. In this respect a Belgian Philistine does not differ from an American Babbitt, a German Philistine is no different from his French counterpart. People who make more than the bare necessities of life, but not enough to meet the demands they accepted without understanding them when they chose to be bourgeois, simply are that way.

From the various strata of the bourgeoisie there stand out diverse types which should be viewed separately. Nobody can know or describe them all; in a single country they are so numerous that a lifetime does not suffice to describe even half of them. To be sure, that would not be an "assignment" for a writer who isn't a pupil, but it would be an assignment, all right; and as far as I am concerned, the paltry visions of well-behaved lit'r'ry fellas interest me far less than reality described by someone in such a way that it is brought quite close to us.

The various strata of the bourgeoisie crystallize certain axioms of which their holders aren't always conscious. In many cases they lead dull lives, unaware of their own selves, just as, in general, the blind spots in people's thoughts are much, much greater than is commonly assumed. Such statements as "There is a God" and "The whale bears its young alive" don't make most people think. They learned these things in school and that is the way it has remained. The axioms I am talking about are articles of faith, of iron construction, accepted in absolute obedience, retaining validity for a lifetime. They haven't been the same at all times. The armor of prejudice with which a citizen of Bremen surrounded himself in 1874 was forged of different plates than that of a Bavarian high-school principal of the year 1928. But they wear this armor until they die and never take it off. They have their vacuums; they divide the world very strictly into large and small print; what is distant gets blurred, and they never get out of the lowlands of their dim cognition. That is the way it has always been. But because nowadays they are ridden by the demon of arrogance who whispers in their ears that he who has technology needs no soul (and, besides, has got one already)—for that reason it is worthwhile to select from the extensive herbarium two plants that I have pressed for myself. What is characteristic of a person is that which he considers a matter of course. Let us take a look.

Frau Emmi Pagel from Guben, Lower Lausitz. Wife of Paul Pagel, bookkeeper, who calls himself a "works official" on his papers. Frau Pagel is of medium height; her legs are a trifle too fat; she has wide hips, a fresh complexion, is well-scrubbed but not well-groomed; she has fat, manicured fingers, with a signet ring and an ornate wedding ring. Hair cut short. By no means a provincial woman, but just a woman who happens to live in a small town.

These are her ten articles of faith:

I. Under the Kaiser everything was better.
II. A head bookkeeper is more than a bookkeeper.
III. A letter mustn't start with " I . . ."; that is impolite.
IV. The Jews are to blame for all the misery. The Jews are dirty, greedy, materialistic, voluptuous, and swarthy. They all have such noses and want to become ministers, provided they aren't already.
V. Of course there are no ghosts. Still, it is uncanny to walk in a cemetery at night or to be in a big dark house alone (Mice).
VI. Servants are a race apart from the propertied, but they don't feel it.
VII. If you put sugar in rhubarb, it turns sour (This item is quite senseless; it stems from a misunderstanding and thus is ineradicable).
VIII. Communism means that everything is chopped to bits. In Russia the women are raped; they murdered a million people there. The Communists want to take everything away from us.
IX. What everybody, including myself, likes is pretty; what everybody, excluding myself, likes is beautiful.
X. The whole world is against Germany—out of envy.

So much for Frau Pagel. On the other hand, Frau Margot Rosenthal, a lawyer's wife, is rather tall, a bit too skinny to be called slender, very well-groomed, but doesn't always look that way. Her hair isn't oily, but you'd think so. As for her complexion . . . "You wouldn't believe all the things I've tried for my . . ."

I. Gentiles are less smart than Jews and that is why they are called "Goyim."
II. Of course there are no ghosts. Still one doesn't have to go to a churchyard alone at night . . . I don't have to try *everything*.
III. Anyone who is able to buy and collect French engravings is cultured.

IV. Communism means that everything is chopped to bits. The Commies want to take away everything it has taken us such trouble to buy, piece by piece. Of course, we've got to have workers and one should treat them decently; the best thing is not to pay any attention to them.

V. The whole world is against the Jews—out of envy.

VI. Art must not be extreme.

VII. Someone who sits in an elegant hotel is elegant himself.

VIII. During a thunderstorm one must turn off the electricity (Cf. Frau Pagel, VII: Rhubarb).

IX. You can't send any husband alone to Paris, least of all mine. The axe in the house . . .

X. My husband is too good-natured.

So much for Frau Rosenthal.
And who will press the other plants?

Harry Zohn

Herr Wendriner Gives a Dinner Party

Good-bye, madam! So long, Mr. Welsch! Have a good trip home, and good night! Bye! . . . Ugh.

What time is it? God, it's a quarter past one! The Mannheimers were going to leave at 12:30, so why did you ask them to stay some more? We've got to cork the red wine, it's still quite good. Whee, am I tired! Did you shut the hall door? Who's there? Oh, it's Marie. Well, Marie, how did you make out? God, close the door. I'm sure Gerolds didn't even tip two marks, that woman is so tight. . . . Vera looked very good tonight, don't you think so? Except for her blackheads; I'm surprised the girl doesn't do anything about them. The keychain? Haven't seen it. You always misplace your keychain. Why don't you look on the night table or in the salon. No, I haven't got it. How often do I have to. . . . Keep your things organized. By the way, I'm not going to invite Aunt Jenny to a dinner party any more. She stuffs herself something awful. These are your relatives! My relatives don't *fress*, they just go bankrupt. Got the keys? Oh, thank God. Just take care of your belongings! The roast hare was pretty good, wasn't it? The ice cream was a bit too soft; the maid will have to watch that. Marschall sure stuck me with that liqueur. He told me it was something special, just for me; that stuff wasn't fit to drink. Well, *they* must have liked it; the bottle's almost empty. Too bad. Where is my cigarette case? Hannah! Hannah! Have you seen my cigarette case? Where's my cigarette case? Someone prob'ly stole it. Sure, where else would it be? Just a minute ago I . . . don't make me nervous! Help me look for it. Such a fine case. Maybe somebody took it along by mistake. . . . Oh, there it is. What are you wrapping up at this time of night? Have the maid do it tomorrow. Come to bed now. By the way, the Regierers seem to know about Oscar; I overheard them telling Lotte at the table, "Old furniture is no dowry!" The nerve! Incidentally, did you ask Dr. Landsmann what you should do about your bronchitis? *I* would have done it without batting an eyelash; that's silly. What's the man a doctor for? I'm not going to invite Jack any more, I'm telling you; he tries to sell insurance to everybody. I don't want any business deals made in my house; you don't do business in a living room. By the way, I talked to Bräunling; he told me that Meyerhold won't take that bunch of shares I told you about. Now stop your wrapping; it's half past one. Got the paper? Fritz says T.W.'s article was awfully good today; I've got to read it. What are all those bottles doing in the toilet? Have them taken out. Now the maid's gone to bed. But you could really have told her to take the bottles out. Where am I supposed to sit now? Hannah! Where's the stock exchange report? It's not in the paper. How could you tell Paul that Meinicke is giving us a special rate? You know that he's going to run there tomorrow, and then Meinicke will give me hell! No, not *you!* Me! That's it. Then don't put the bottles there. Help me pick them up. The whole bathtub is green; those stains will never come out. Those dinner parties! They'll come out; don't make such a fuss. It must have cost at least two hundred marks, all together. No, I don't care to be invited! Do I get my hard-earned money back that way? Besides, the Siegels never invite you back—one time a child is sick, then they don't have a maid; I'd like to have so many excuses some time! No more parties for the next two months! That's final. Come on now, I've got to get up early in the morning; hurry up and go to bed. I'll be up in a minute; I just want to read that article. Don't step into that. I'm glad that vacations are coming; I can't stand the sight of all of them any more. Well, at Garmisch we'll be left in peace. The Meyerholds will be there too; the Welschs are coming and so is old Regierer. Lotte may bring along Grete. This way at least we'll have someone to turn to down there. Hannah! Hannah! We're out of toilet paper again! That bunch even used up our toilet paper! Never mind, I'll use the newspaper . . . !

Harry Zohn

Herr Wendriner in Paris

Mornin', Welsch! So what's new? Yes, we're back again. Since day before yesterday. Come on in. Well, first to the Riviera and then a little side trip to Paris. How was it—? God . . . ya know . . . ya know: Paris ain't so . . . I mean, sure, some things there are faabulous. Have a cigar?

So when we get there, it's raining cats 'n dogs. I'm thinking: just my luck. That's right: ten minutes we had to wait for a cab, and the guy didn't understand at first, till I, you know, then everything was fine. I had 'em reserve me a room—The Grong Hotel, not bad. Right, so the next morning we get started. First I show my wife around Paris. No, never been there before. They got boulevards though—lemme tell ya, faabulous traffic, I mean, incredible. The cars are lined up six, eight lanes across. Unbelievable! And those guys can drive—! You keep thinkin', they're gonna flip over, or you're gonna trip or fall. But nobody flips over. Oh and by the way, Regierer was in Paris too—met him at the Plass doola Opra; sure was glad to see him, he'd just gotten the latest market figures cabled straight from Berlin, always nice to hear news from home. He, listen, don't drop the ashes on the carpet, the wife'd have a fit, here's an ashtray! So my wife went shopping, there was no holding her back. All that cheap, you know, Paris isn't either! I bought her among other things a suit and two dresses, a full length evening gown, and then something for the beach, which, God willing, she'll wear at Heringsdorf—for the whole lot all in all I paid 3550 francs, that makes, wait a minute, at that time it was . . . about 510 marks. Well for that kind of money she can get it in Berlin too. But very chic. And such a chic salesgirl took care of us, you wouldn't believe it . . . Naturally we ate at Prooneers. You ever eat at Prooneers? No? It's faabulous, lemme tell ya. A very high-class clientele—Englishmen, big-shot Americans, obviously a lot of diplomatic brass too. At Sheerocks? No, I didn't get there, it's not supposed to be that good. In general I find the portions are a little small, sure the ordoovers are fantastic, but the portions *are* a little small. A friend of my wife's brother has a cousin who lives in Paris, he took us to a place foreigners don't usually get to, it was authentic Parisian. So then we went to the Loover, very interesting, you ever been to the Loover yourself?, it's a must, of course. So then, you know, we just sort of walked around, in the evening we caught a show, saw Mustangette. You ever see Mustangette? Oh, you did . . . well yeah, she's not so hot. But the show was faabulous. And then we saw this artiste at a little theater, can't recall what her name was . . . I can't remember her name . . . you wouldn't've heard of her—well she was simply faabulous. Never saw anything like it. I didn't think the neon lights were such a big deal, I mean, we've got the same in Berlin too. Next evening we were up at Mongmarter—you know the place? Oh, you do, huh . . . yeah, I wasn't so crazy about it either. You don't even see any Bohemians around. But then we went to the Parakeet—you know it? You don't know that place? You mean, you've never been to the Parakeet? Well, it's just faabulous! We paid, wait a minute, champagne of course, all in all it came to 320 francs. That makes . . . that was 45 marks at the time. The Cafe de Paree? Oh really, you were there? No, I didn't go there, it's not supposed to be anything really. And then we bumped into the Freunds, we were buying stockings for my wife, just standing around outside, figuring out the rate of exchange, and who do you think was standing right next to us? Freund. With the Mrs. I don't particularly care for him, you know. By the way, did he get that credit from Stuttgart? Listen, lemme tell ya something: that guy is an out and out crook! He knew damn well I wanted the credit, after all, weren't we the first to negotiate with those people? . . . Speaking of which, he doesn't look well. Regierer stayed at the Clarrich—I'd like to know how that guy can affort it. What else did we see? Prooneers, the shows, the big opra house, Mongmarter, Noter Dame, the Loover—all the main sights. There's not much else to see really.

Oh yeah, and then one evening I went out alone. You know what I'm sayin' . . . so first I looked up Dr. Tucholsky, yeah, the one that always writes those Berlin things in the *Weltbuehne*. Every time I read that stuff, I says to my wife: "Just like Regierer" Well of course he was delighted to see me, always glad to see the folks from back home. Yeah. So and then I asked him for some addresses. Not at all—I'm a *Weltbuehne* subscriber, why not? He claimed he didn't know any . . . well Regierer knew a couple, and the fellas at the stock exchange had told me about some others—so one evening I says to my wife, honey, you must be tired, rest up a bit, I'm goin' out a while to have a look at the show windows. So we took a cab, Regierer and me, it seemed too risky to go there alone. Well, get a load o' this . . . I get there, see, and there's a bunch o' guys standing around outside, I push my way by, all of a sudden I hear somebody say, "Krauts!"—well I don't poke around where I'm not wanted, and just as I'm about to move on, suddenly I hear, those guys are speaking German! Well I went over to him and I told him a thing or two! Germans on vacation, you know what I'm sayin' . . . well I let him have it. He was a little guy too, I sure told him! So inside the place there were mirrors all around and a hall full of naked broads. A whole hall full. No touching naturally. Course I paid for the obligatory bottle of champagne, and the girls danced a little, one of them came on to me, a very nice girl, and she spoke a little German too. To tell you the truth though, I was a bit disappointed. I thought for sure the Parisian girls had more class. Besides, I ask you: where's all that famous Paris glitter? Sure you might catch a chic number or two on the big boulevards—but nothing you wouldn't find at a gala opening back home. Lemme tell ya something: it's all a lot o' hooey. Y'understand? A lot o' hooey. That's what I say. On Tuesday then we left. My wife wanted to stay a little longer. But I says to her, I says, sweetheart—enough is enough. I've had my fill of Paris.

And I'll tell ya somethin' else, Welsch—for God's sake, will you quit dropping ashes on the carpet! You do that kind o' thing at home? The nerve! But I'll tell ya somethin': sure I like to travel. But you know, after you've been away on vacation for so long, always at the tables, every evening at those elegant casino's down on the Riviera—well after customs, soon as the train rolls across the border, and you spot your first station attendants in their Prussian blue—and you've got your peace and your German sense of order back again after all that to-do—Paris here, Paris there—say what you like—: there's no place like home—!

Peter Wortsman

Herr Wendriner Can't Fall Asleep

For God's sake, can't that woman lie still! Some women sleep as soon as you put them to bed, and they stay asleep too! Will you lie still already! If I turn out the light, you won't lie still either. Alright—I'll turn it off.

. . . Impossible to fall asleep. I don't know what it is. Couldn't be the beer I had this evening, didn't smoke today either—have to talk to Friedman about it sometime. Sports! he's always saying—got to get into sports! Maybe play soccer together on the Kurfuerstendamm . . . ridiculous! Haven't yet paid that last bill of his either, come to think of it—so, let him wait. Others wait too. What was that joke he just told me the other day . . . ? Oh yeah—"Say: Aah, sir!" Terrific joke, have to tell it to Welsch tomorrow, that guy gets such a kick out of a good joke . . . What kind of headlight is that . . . fire engine? Nah, car . . . Good cars in Berlin these days, just try to find cars like that in Paris, I always say; London cars not worth much either. What's this itching me here all the time? Now I . . . God, I was going to take a shower this evening, plain forgot . . . Tomorrow, then. No—no time tomorrow either—alright, tomorrow evening. It's not like I'm going courting. 45,000 in two years at 18 percent, that makes . . . 18 percent—those people are out of their minds . . . That's the word. 'amorphous'—Lucie wanted to know it for her crossword puzzle, was running through my head at work all morning—strange, the things that sometimes go through your head. Freutel was supposed to show me the balance sheet on Esmarch & Ehrmann—again he forgot—person ought to keep a notepad by his bed—put one there tomorrow . . . leg itches me like crazy. What a paunch!—

Getting fat. When I still had that little thing going with Grete, always used to tickle me in bed, said: 'So, fatty dear . . . ?' Yeah.— You asleep already . . . ? Always asleep. Well, after all, we're not children anymore. Where's that water—I'll have a little water to drink. Almost!—watch almost fell. What's tomorrow evening—? Got to stay late at the office tomorrow, catch up on some work, Tuesday, Wednesday . . . day after tomorrow we're going to the Regierers', Trude's coming too, wants to get the word on that Persian rug—getting it real cheap . . . that Joey of theirs is an unruly brat, tell his father next chance I get, don't see why not—Friday we've got tickets to the opera, be at the Bristol afterwards—Saturday's the fashion show, she sure conned me into that one . . . All I care about's the mocha . . . Really ought to relax. No sense even thinking about relaxing now—not till July at the earliest . . . maybe go to Bolzano, heard a lot of good things about Bolzano . . . Father always wanted so much to go to Bolzano . . . never got there . . . What's that smell . . . ? Didn't I tell Hanni I will not have that perfume around here anymore . . . awful perfume! If I hadn't felt so sorry for Oscar, never would've bought it off him. Never amounted to much in life, that fellow. A man's got to amount to something. I have . . . hold it, let me figure it out: a hundred and thirty thousand in the business, four thousand at home, then there's the twenty thousand Benno owes me, good as cash . . . Fritz says I ought to read Magic Mountain. He can talk. Hardly get to read anymore. Haven't even read the Memoirs of Wagner I got for Christmas. No time for anything anymore. Think about death a lot these days. Nonsense. Still I do think a lot about death. That comes from bad digestion. No, it doesn't come from bad digestion. You get older, that's all. How long've we been married now . . . ? Well, she's taken care of, at least that much I've managed, thank God. Wait till I'm dead, they'll start realizing what a gem they had in me. A man gets far too little recognition in his life. Afterwards it's too late. Let them cry then. Old Leppschitzer drew quite a crowd. I'll have at least that many . . . Maid's just getting home—at this hour! She could shut the door a little more quietly too . . . What's a girl like that do evenings? Goes to see her girl friends . . . Well, Emma's got a fiancé. Not a bad-looking girl really! Still has it all up front—will you lie still already! What do people like that think of us? Probably swear all hell about their bosses when they get together evenings. None of that Bolshevik bull when I was an apprentice. Boy did we ever have to work . . . haha—when I think back how we glued old Buchowetzki's scissors to the table . . . And he tugged and tugged and couldn't get 'em loose—haha! But they'll sure cry when I'm gone. Say what you want—Stresemann gave some speech the other day at the economic conference. The bromide doesn't help much either anymore—maybe I took it too early. What—? Nothing. It was nothing. Just a loose spring in the mattress . . .

Terrible, when you can't fall asleep. When you can't fall asleep, you're all alone. Don't like being alone. Got to have people around me, activity, family, work . . . When I'm all by myself: when I'm all by myself, then there's nobody. And then I'm all alone. Back itches. It's always like this. Any second now I'll fall asleep . . . well then, good n'—"

Peter Wortsman

Gedichte

Park Monceau

Hier ist es hübsch. Hier kann ich ruhig träumen.
Hier bin ich Mensch—und nicht nur Zivilist.
Hier darf ich links gehn. Unter grünen Bäumen
sagt keine Tafel, was verboten ist.

Ein dicker Kullerball liegt auf dem Rasen.
Ein Vogel zupft an einem hellen Blatt.
Ein kleiner Junge gräbt sich in der Nasen
und freut sich, wenn er was gefunden hat.

Es prüfen vier Amerikanerinnen,
ob Cook auch recht hat und hier Bäume stehn.
Paris von außen und Paris von innen:
sie sehen nichts und müssen alles sehn.

Die Kinder lärmen auf den bunten Steinen.
Die Sonne scheint und glitzert auf ein Haus.
Ich sitze still und lasse mich bescheinen
und ruh von meinem Vaterlande aus.

Poems

Poetry translated by Karl F. Ross

Parc Monceau

A charming spot—so peaceful and idyllian.
Beneath the trees I dream in sheer delight.
Here I'm a man—not merely a civilian;
no sign here says: "Verboten" or "Keep Right."

A sparrow plucks a petal from a posy.
A rubber ball lands rolling in a ditch.
A little fellow picks his little nosie
and looks delighted when he strikes it rich.

Four Yankee ladies busily examine
if Cook's is right and trees adorn this place;
they search through Paris with touristic famine
and see its sights but do not find its face.

The sun is bright and glitters on a shingle.
The children shout and frolic in the sand.
I bask in sunshine, with my nerves atingle,
and take a respite from my fatherland.

An einen Bonzen

Einmal waren wir beide gleich.
Beide: Proleten im deutschen Kaiserreich.
Beide in derselben Luft,
beide in gleicher verschwitzter Kluft;
dieselbe Werkstatt—derselbe Lohn—
derselbe Meister—dieselbe Fron—
beide dasselbe elende Küchenloch . . .
    Genosse, erinnerst du dich noch?

Aber du, Genosse, warst flinker als ich.
Dich drehen—das konntest du meisterlich.
Wir mußten leiden, ohne zu klagen,
aber du,—du konntest es sagen.
Kanntest die Bücher und die Broschüren,
wußtest besser die Feder zu führen.
Treue um Treue—wir glaubten dir doch!
    Genosse, erinnerst du dich noch?

Heute ist das alles vergangen.
Man kann nur durchs Vorzimmer zu dir gelangen.
Du rauchst nach Tisch die dicken Zigarren,
du lachst über Straßenhetzer und Narren.
Weißt nichts mehr von alten Kameraden,
wirst aber überall eingeladen.
Du zuckst die Achseln beim Hennessy
und vertrittst die deutsche Sozialdemokratie.
Du hast mit der Welt deinen Frieden gemacht.
Hörst du nicht manchmal in dunkler Nacht
eine leise Stimme, die mahnend spricht:
    «Genosse, schämst du dich nicht—?»

To a Socialist Bigwig

Once we were equal, you and me,
workers in Germany's monarchy;
breathing both the same rotten air,
both with nothing but rags to wear.
The same old sweatshop, the same hard boss,
the same low wages, the same heavy cross.
The same dark kitchen, that filthy den—
    Comrade, remember when?

But you, my friend, were more skillful and quick.
Getting out from under—you mastered that trick.
We toiled and suffered, we had no choice;
but you were able to raise your voice.
When it came to writing, you did even better;
the books and pamphlets you knew to the letter.
A pledge for a pledge, we trusted you then—
    Comrade, remember when?

Now all that is past. Your manners grew snobby.
To see you, one has to wait in the lobby.
While taking food and cigars from the waiters,
you scoff at hotheads and agitators.
Accepting all sorts of invitations,
you shun old buddies and associations.
You shrug as you sip champagne from your glass—
a spokesman for Germany's working class!
You have abandoned our common fight.
Haven't you ever heard, in the night,
a small inner voice, calling softly your name:
    "Comrade—have you no shame?"

Die Deplacierten

Uns haben sie, glaub ich, falsch geboren.
Von wegen Ort und wegen Zeit
sind wir verdattert und verloren
und fluchen unsrer Einsamkeit.

Warum, Mama, grad an der Panke?
Warum nicht fünfzig Jahr zurück?
Wie schlecht placiert wuchs der Gedanke
zu eurem jungen Liebesglück!

Warum nicht lieber auf dem Sunda-
Eiländchen 1810?
Doch hier und heut? Das ist kein Wunda—
das kann ja nicht in Ordnung gehn!

Warum nicht in Australien hausend?
Warum nicht Fürst von Erzerum?
Warum nicht erst im Jahr Zweitausend?
Weshalb? Wieso? Woher? Warum?

Der Weltkrieg. Lebensroße Zeiten.
Der Bankkommis als Offizier.
Brotkarten. Morde. Grenzen. Pleiten.
Und alles ausgerechnet wir.

Schraub hoch dein Karma wie die Inder.
Bleibt auch für uns nur noch Verzicht:
Wenn meine und sie kriegt mal Kinder—
In Deutschland darf sie nicht.

Misplaced Persons

Methinks that we were born in error,
both as to time and as to place.
We live in loneliness and terror
and curse the fate we have to face.

Why, Ma, this side of the Atlantic?
Why not some fifty years ago?
How poorly planned was your romantic
anent the fruits it was to grow!

Why not down on the Lesser Sunda
Isles, say, in eighteen-hundred ten?
But here and now? It is no wonder
that things got messy there and then!

Why not far south of the equator?
Why not a prince in Travancore?
Why not a hundred summers later?
Why not? How come? Wherefrom? What for?

World War—resounding proclamations.
As officers the office clerks.
Bankruptcies. Murders. Borders. Rations.
And just for us—we got the works.

So let us practice, like a lama,
self-discipline for you and me:
My love, you want to be a mamma?
No—not in Germany!

Der Graben

Mutter, wozu hast du deinen aufgezogen?
Hast dich zwanzig Jahr mit ihm gequält?
Wozu ist er dir in deinen Arm geflogen,
und du hast ihm leise was erzählt?
    Bis sie ihn dir weggenommen haben,
    Für den Graben, Mutter, für den Graben.

Junge, kannst du noch an Vater denken?
Vater nahm dich oft auf seinen Arm.
Und er wollt dir einen Groschen schenken,
und er spielte mit dir Räuber und Gendarm.
    Bis sie ihn dir weggenommen haben.
    Für den Graben, Junge, für den Graben.

Drüben die französischen Genossen
lagen dicht bei Englands Arbeitsmann.
Alle haben sie ihr Blut vergossen,
und zerschossen ruht heut Mann bei Mann.
    Alte Leute, Männer, mancher Knabe
    in dem einen großen Massengrabe.

Seid nicht stolz auf Orden und Geklunker!
Seid nicht stolz auf Narben und die Zeit!
In die Gräben schickten euch die Junker,
Staatswahn und der Fabrikantenneid.
    Ihr wart gut genug zum Fraß für Raben,
    Für das Grab, Kamraden, für den Graben!

Werft die Fahnen fort! Die Militärkapellen
spielen auf zu euerm Todestanz.
Seid ihr hin: ein Kranz von Immortellen—
das ist dann der Dank des Vaterlands.
    Denkt an Todesröcheln und Gestöhne.
    Drüben stehen Väter, Mütter, Söhne,
    schuften schwer, wie ihr, ums bißchen Leben.
    Wollt ihr denen nicht die Hände geben?
    Reicht die Bruderhand als schönste aller Gaben
    übern Graben, Leute, übern Graben—!

The Trench

Mother, why have you brought up your fellow,
taught and tended him for twenty years,
waited anxiously to hear his "hello,"
whispered little stories in his ears?
   Till they hauled him from his bed and bench
   to the trench, good woman, to the trench.

Sonny, do you still remember Daddy?
How he used to take you on his arm,
how he gave a penny to his laddie
and he chased with you around the farm?
   Till they sent him out to fight the French
   in the trench, young fellow, in the trench.

France's comrades over there were lying
side by side with England's workingmen.
Old and young ones, even boys, fell dying
where the bullets hit them, there and then.
   As their lifeblood ebbed, the soil to drench,
   they were buried in that common trench.

Don't be proud of chevrons and citations!
Don't be proud of medals and awards!
You stood guard for greedy corporations,
pseudo-statesmen and the feudal lords.
   Yours was just the squalor and the stench
   of the tomb, companions, and the trench!

Dump those flags! A dance of death they're casting
to the music of an army band.
When you're gone—a wreath of everlasting,
that's the thank-you from your fatherland.
   Think what agony you cause to others:
   Over there stand fathers, sons and mothers,
   struggling hard, like you, for meager living—
   won't you turn to them without misgiving?
   Stretch your hand out, let your fist unclench,
   'cross the trench, my friends, across the trench!

Ideal und Wirklichkeit

In stiller Nacht und monogamen Betten
denkst du dir aus, was dir am Leben fehlt.
Die Nerven knistern. Wenn wir das doch hätten,
was uns, weil es nicht da ist, leise quält.
    Du präparierst dir im Gedankengange
    das, was du willst—und nachher kriegst dus nie . . .
    Man möchte immer eine große Lange,
    Und dann bekommt man eine kleine Dicke—
        C'est la vie—!

Sie muß sich wie in einem Kugellager
in ihren Hüften biegen, groß und blond.
Ein Pfund zu wenig—und sie wäre mager,
wer je in diesen Haaren sich gesonnt . . .
    Nachher erliegst du dem verfluchten Hange,
    der Eile und der Phantasie.
    Man möchte immer eine große Lange,
    und dann bekommt man eine kleine Dicke—
        Ssälawih—!

Man möchte eine helle Pfeife kaufen
und kauft die dunkle—andere sind nicht da.
Man möchte jeden Morgen dauerlaufen
und tut es nicht. Beinah . . . beinah . . .
    Wir dachten unter kaiserlichem Zwange
    an eine Republik . . . und nun ists die!
    Man möchte immer eine große Lange,
    und dann bekommt man eine kleine Dicke—
        Ssälawih—!

Ideal and Reality

In dead of night and monogamic bedding
you brood about the pleasures that you miss.
You toss and turn. Your nervous itch is spreading.
What are the thoughts that torment you like this?
   You visualize in your imagination
   the things you want—yet which will never be . . .
   One always wishes for a trim and tall one
   and then one winds up with a fat and small one—
     C'est la vie!

The one you dream of must be young and eager
and swing and swivel freely in her hips.
Take off a pound—and you might call her meager;
what flaming hair to match her scarlet lips!
   But then you yield to that accursed sensation,
   to haste and to the lure of phantasy.
   One always wishes for a trim and tall one,
   And then one winds up with a fat and small one—
     Cellarvee!

You want a meerschaum pipe, all white and pearly,
and buy a black one—it was all they had.
You want to do ten push-ups, bright and early,
but put it off. Too bad . . . too bad . . .
   We hankered under Kaiser's domination
   for a republic—now we have one, see?
   One always wishes for a trim and tall one
   and then one winds up with a fat and small one—
     Cellarvee!

Der andre Mann

Du lernst ihn in einer Gesellschaft kennen.
Er plaudert. Er ist zu dir nett.
Er kann dir alle Tenniscracks nennen.
Er sieht gut aus. Ohne Fett.
    Er tanzt ausgezeichnet. Du siehst ihn dir an . . .
Dann tritt zu euch beiden dein Mann.

Und du vergleichst sie in deinem Gemüte.
Dein Mann kommt nicht gut dabei weg.
Wie er schon dasteht—du liebe Güte!
Und hinten am Hals der Speck!
    Und du denkst bei dir so: «Eigentlich . . .
Der da wäre ein Mann für mich!»

Ach, gnädige Frau! Hör auf einen wahren
und guten alten Papa!
Hättst du den Neuen: in ein, zwei Jahren
ständest du ebenso da!
    Dann kennst du seine Nuancen beim Kosen;
    dann kennst du ihn in Unterhosen;
    dann wird er satt in deinem Besitze;
    dann kennst du alle seine Witze.
    Dann siehst du ihn in Freude und Zorn,
    von oben und unten, von hinten und vorn . . .
Glaub mir: wenn man uns näher kennt,
gibt sich das mit dem happy end.
Wir sind manchmal reizend, auf einer Feier . . .
und den Rest des Tages ganz wie Herr Meyer.
Beurteil uns nie nach den besten Stunden.

Und hast du einen Kerl gefunden,
mit dem man einigermaßen auskommen kann:
    dann bleib bei dem eigenen Mann!

The Other Man

You happen to meet him at a dinner.
You start conversing with him.
He knows the name of each Davis Cup winner.
He looks attractive. And slim.
    He dances superbly. His face is clean.
    And then your husband appears on the scene.

You measure one man against the other.
Your husband comes off second-best:
What a disgusting figure—oh brother!
So paunchy! So sloppily dressed!
    And you say to yourself: Why, certainly
    that one would be a man for me.

Now, lady, I may sound irritating
but what I tell you is true:
You'd give that other the same low rating
just after a year or two.
    By then you know his technique of caressing;
    you've seen him in every stage of undressing.
    He then has his fill of your affection;
    you've heard all the jokes in his collection;
    you have observed him in joy and in fear,
    from top and bottom, from front and rear . . .
believe me, the more one sees of us,
the less one finds us glamorous.
We may be charming at a party
and other times just like Joey or Marty.
Don't fall for those Sunday faces we carry—

and if the fellow you chose to marry
is someone with whom you can get by,
then—take my advice—hold on to the guy!

Danach

Es wird nach einem happy end
im Film jewöhnlich abjeblendt.
 Man sieht bloß noch in ihre Lippen
 den Helden seinen Schnurrbart stippen—
 da hat sie nu den Schentelmen.
  Na, un denn—?

Denn jehn die Beeden brav ins Bett.
Na ja . . . diß is ja auch janz nett.
 A manchmal möcht man doch jern wissn:
 Wat tun se, wenn se sich nich kissn?
 Die könn ja doch nich imma penn . . . !
  Na, un denn—?

Denn säuselt im Kamin der Wind.
Denn kricht det junge Paar'n Kind.
 Denn kocht sie Milch. Die Milch looft üba.
 Denn macht er Krach. Denn weent sie drüba.
 Denn wolln sich beede jänzlich trenn . . .
  Na, un denn—?

Denn is det Kind nich uffn Damm.
Denn bleihm die beeden doch zesamm.
 Denn quäln se sich noch manche Jahre.
 Er will noch wat mit blonde Haare:
 vorn dof und hinten minorenn . . .
  Na, un denn—?

Denn sind se alt. Der Sohn haut ab.
Der Olle macht nu ooch bald schlapp.
 Vajessen Kuß und Schnurrbartzeit—
 Ach, Menschenskind, wie liecht det weit!
 Wie der noch scharf uff Muttern war,
 det is schon beinah nich mehr wahr!

Afterward

Most movies, in their final scene,
fade happy-ending from the screen.
One briefly sees the lady's lips
brushed by the hero's mustache tips.
So now, at last, they'll tie the knot—
and then what?

Then, after being duly wed,
they have a little fun in bed.
The only thing one asks is this:
What's going on when they don't kiss?
They can't be always on the cot. . . .
And then what?

Then seasons change and time moves on.
The little woman bears a son.
The milk boils over. Tempers rise.
He cusses her. She wipes her eyes.
He wants to leave her on the spot—
and then what?

Then junior gets the chicken pox;
that keeps the marriage off the rocks.
The years go by. He has a fling
once with a silly little thing,
a pretty redhead, young and hot—
and then what?

Then they are old. The son checks out.
How long can Pop still move about?
Forgotten kiss and mustache days—
it's all so distant, in a haze.
The time he had a crush on her:
When in the world did that occur?

Der olle Mann denkt so zurück:
Wat hat er nu von seinen Jlück?
Die Ehe war zum jrößten Teile
vabrühte Milch un Langeweile.
Und darum wird beim happy end
im Film jewöhnlich abjeblendt.

Der Zerstreute

Mein Blinddarn, der ruht in Palmnicken;
ein Backenzahn und überdies
ein Milchzahn liegen in Saarbrücken.
Die Mandeln ruhen in Paris.

So streu ich mich trotz hohen Zöllen
weit durch Europa hin durchs Land.
Auch hat die Klinik in Neukölln
noch etwas Nasenscheidewand.

Ein guter Arzt will operieren.
Es freut ihn, und es bringt auch Geld.
Viel ist nicht mehr zu amputieren.
Ich bin zu gut für diese Welt.

Was soll ich armes Luder machen,
wenn die Posaune blasen mag?
Wie tret ich an mit meinen sieben Sachen
am heiligen Auferstehungstag?

Der liebe Gott macht nicht viel Federlesen.
«Herr Tiger!» ruft er. «Komm hervor!
Wie siehst du aus, lädiertes Wesen?
Und wo—wo hast du den Humor?»

The old one thinks about his past:
His happiness had faded fast.
Their married life was largely filled
with boredom and with milk that spilled.
That's why the happy end, on screen,
comes mostly as the final scene.

Split Personality

They severed my appendix in Bavaria;
a molar was abandoned on the Rhine.
In every place, despite the customs barrier,
I leave behind some little part of mine.

French doctors took my tonsils out and kept 'em—
it seems I've spread my body rather thin—
and, come to think of it, a piece of septum
lies somewhere in my hometown of Berlin.

A surgeon likes to do an operation
that satisfies and brings him money's worth.
Not much is left of me for amputation;
I simply am too perfect for this earth.

What can I do, a wrack among the creatures,
the day I hear that Final Trumpet sound?
What will I say about those missing features
when yonder Day of Judgment rolls around?

So there I stand, to be adjudicated.
"Herr T.!" the Lord will call "step forth, my son!
You look so dreary and dilapidated,
and where—where has your sense of humor gone?"

«Ich las»—sag ich dann ohne Bangen—
«einst den Etat der deutschen Generalität.
Da ist mir der Humor vergangen.»
Und Gott versteht.
                    Und Gott versteht.

Europa

Am Rhein, da wächst ein süffiger Wein—
der darf aber nicht nach England hinein—
    Buy British!
In Wien gibt es herrliche Torten und Kuchen,
die haben in Schweden nichts zu suchen—
    Köp svenska varor!
In Italien verfaulen die Apfelsinen—
laß die deutsche Landwirtschaft verdienen!
    Deutsche, kauft deutsche Zitronen!
Und auf jedem Quadratkilometer Raum
träumt einer seinen völkischen Traum.
Und leise flüstert der Wind durch die Bäume . . .
    Räume sind Schäume.

Da liegt Europa. Wie sieht es aus?
Wie ein bunt angestrichnes Irrenhaus.
Die Nationen schuften auf Rekord:
    Export! Export!
Die andern! Die andern sollen kaufen!
Die andern sollen die Weine saufen!
Die andern sollen die Schiffe heuern!
Die andern sollen die Kohlen verfeuern!
Wir?
    Zollhaus, Grenzpfahl und Einfuhrschein:
wir lassen nicht das geringste herein.
Wir nicht. Wir haben ein Ideal:
Wir hungern. Aber streng national.

"Sir," I'll reply, "I read some press releases
about the budget of our high command;
that's when my sense of humor went to pieces."
And God will nod.
                    And God will understand.

Europe 1932

Tall grows the vine along the Rhine—
but England may not drink that wine—
    Britons, buy British!
The Austrians make delicious cake
of which a Swede must not partake—
    Swedes, buy Swedish goods!
Italian citrus crops decay
so German farmers can make more hay—
    Germans, buy German lemons!
And on every square mile of territory
they dream of home-grown national glory.
Whispers the wind from London to Rome . . .
    Home, sweet foam!

There you have Europe, looking quaint:
a madhouse colored with motley paint.
At record rates its goods are made
    for the export trade!
The others should buy the merchandise!
The others should eat the apple pies!
The others should hire the steamship fleet!
The others should fire the coal and peat!
We?
    Import license and customs gate:
a barrier nothing must penetrate.
Not us! We have an ideal, we say:
We starve. But strictly the national way.

Fahnen und Hymnen an allen Ecken.
Europa? Europa soll doch verrecken!
Und wenn alles der Pleite entgegentreibt:
daß nur die Nation erhalten bleibt!
Menschen braucht es nicht mehr zu geben.
England! Polen! Italien muß leben!
Der Staat frißt uns auf. Ein Gespenst. Ein Begriff.
Der Staat, das ist ein Ding mitm Pfiff.
Das Ding ragt auf bis zu den Sternen—
von dem kann noch die Kirche was lernen.
Jeder soll kaufen. Niemand kann kaufen.
Es rauchen die völkischen Scheiterhaufen.
Es lodern die völkischen Opferfeuer:
Der Sinn des Lebens ist die Steuer!
Der Himmel sei unser Konkursverwalter!
Die Neuzeit tanzt als Mittelalter.

Die Nation ist das achte Sakrament—!
Gott segne diesen Kontinent.

Anthems and flags on every spot.
What about Europe? Europe may rot!
Everything else can go to hell
As long as the Nation is doing well!
People? Who cares if they survive—
Britain! Italy! Poland must thrive!
The State devours us. A specter, a myth.
The State, that's a thing to be reckoned with.
The thing grows skyward into the blue—
there even the Church can learn something new.
Come all and buy! Yet there are no buyers.
Up flare the tribal funeral pyres.
Glow, tribal fires of immolation:
the goal of existence is the taxation.
Let Heaven be our estate's receiver:
this age has medieval fever.

The State becomes a sacrament—
may God protect this Continent!

Erich Kästner

Die andre Möglichkeit

Wenn wir den Krieg gewonnen hätten,
mit Wogenprall und Sturmgebraus,
dann wäre Deutschland nicht zu retten
und gliche einem Irrenhaus.

Man würde uns nach Noten zähmen
wie einen wilden Völkerstamm.
Wir sprängen, wenn Sergeanten kämen,
vom Trottoir und stünden stramm.

Wenn wir den Krieg gewonnen hätten,
dann wären wir ein stolzer Staat.
Und preßten noch in unsern Betten
die Hände an die Hosennaht.

Die Frauen müßten Kinder werfen.
Ein Kind im Jahre. Oder Haft.
Der Staat braucht Kinder als Konserven.
Und Blut schmeckt ihm wie Himbeersaft.

Wenn wir den Krieg gewonnen hätten,
dann wär der Himmel national.
Die Pfarrer trügen Epauletten.
Und Gott wär deutscher General.

Erich Kästner

The Other Possibility

If we had won the war with waving
of flags and roaring, if we had,
then Germany would be past saving,
then Germany would have gone mad.

One would attempt to make us tame
like savage tribes that one might mention.
We'd leave the sidewalk if a sergeant came
and stand attention.

If we had won the war of late
we'd be a proud and headstrong state
and press in bed in our dreams
our hands to our trouser seams.

Women must bear, each woman serves
a child a year. Or calaboose.
The state needs children as preserves,
and it swills blood like berry juice.

If we had won the war, I bet
that heaven would be national,
the clergy would wear epaulets,
God be a German general.

Die Grenze wär ein Schützengraben.
Der Mond wär ein Gefreitenknopf.
Wir würden einen Kaiser haben
und einen Helm statt einem Kopf.

Wenn wir den Krieg gewonnen hätten,
dann wäre jedermann Soldat.
Ein Volk der Laffen und Lafetten!
Und ringsherum wär Stacheldraht!

Dann würde auf Befehl geboren.
Weil Menschen ziemlich billig sind.
Und weil man mit Kanonenrohren
allein die Kriege nicht gewinnt.

Dann läge die Vernunft in Ketten.
Und stünde stündlich vor Gericht.
Und Kriege gäb's wie Operetten.
Wenn wir den Kriege gewonnen hätten—
zum Glück gewannen wir ihn nicht.

Jahrgang 1899

Wir haben die Frauen zu Bett gebracht,
als die Männer in Frankreich standen.
Wir hatten uns das viel schöner gedacht.
Wir waren nur Konfirmanden.

Dann holte man uns zum Militär,
bloß so als Kanonenfutter.
In der Schule wurden die Bänke leer,
zu Hause weinte die Mutter.

Trenches would take the place of borders.
No moon, insignia instead.
An emperor would issue orders.
We'd have a helmet and no head.

If we had won, then everyone
would be a soldier; the entire
land would be run by goon and gun,
and all around would be barbed wire.

On order, women would throw twins,
for men cost hardly more than stone,
and above all one cannot win
a war with guns alone.

Then reason would be kept in fetters,
accused and always on the spot.
And wars would come like operettas.
If we had won the last war—but
we were in luck and we did not.

Note: This poem, written after World War roman numeral one, in addition to attracting understandable and obvious enmities, also attracted
some unsuspected enemies. The "we were in luck" of the last line was
taken for a shout of jubilation, when in fact it was a very, very bitter observation. Now we have lost yet another war and the poem will continue
to be misunderstood.—E.K.

Walter Kaufmann

Born in 1899

The men were fighting in France in the war;
we took care of their wives in their stead.
It was not the thrill we had bargained for.
We were fifteen and took them to bed.

Then we were of the proper age,
were drafted as cannon fodder to die.
Classrooms were emptied as we reached that stage,
while mothers were left home to cry.

Dann gab es ein bißchen Revolution
und schneite Kartoffelflocken;
dann kamen die Frauen, wie früher schon,
und dann kamen die Gonokokken.

Inzwischen verlor der Alte sein Geld,
da wurden wir Nachtstudenten.
Bei Tag waren wir bureau-angestellt
und rechneten mit Prozenten.

Dann hätte sie fast ein Kind gehabt,
ob von dir, ob von mir—was weiß ich!
Das hat ihr ein Freund von uns ausgeschabt.
Und nächstens werden wir Dreißig.

Wir haben sogar ein Examen gemacht
und das meiste schon wieder vergessen.
Jetzt sind wir allein bei Tag und bei Nacht
und haben nichts Rechtes zu fressen!

Wir haben der Welt in die Schnauze geguckt,
anstatt mit Puppen zu spielen.
Wir haben der Welt auf die Weste gespuckt,
soweit wir vor Ypern nicht fielen.

Man hat unsern Körper und hat unsern Geist
ein wenig zu wenig gekräftigt.
Man hat uns zu lange, zu früh und zumeist
in der Weltgeschichte beschäftigt!

Die Alten behaupten, es würde nun Zeit
für uns zum Säen und Ernten.
Noch einen Moment. Bald sind wir bereit.
Noch einen Moment. Bald ist es so weit!
Dann zeigen wir euch, was wir lernten!

Some revolution then ended the war.
Potato flakes made up every meal.
We bedded the women just as before,
With gonorrhea thrown into the deal.

Meanwhile the old man had lost his dough,
we were part of the night-study scene,
while every day to some office we'd go,
involved in accounting routine.

And then she was pregnant, and who was to blame?
Was I the child's father, or could it be you?
A friend saw to it that the kid never came.
Soon I'll be thirty, and you'll be too.

They even gave us diplomas, it's true,
but little we learned we'd retain.
Now we feel lonely and empty and blue,
and hungry to eat once again.

At our old planet we took a close glance,
when we should have played on the nursery floor.
We spit at the world and took our chance,
except for those guys who were killed in the war.

We had always too little to grow really strong
and healthy in body and mind.
We were busy too early, too much and too long
with the history of mankind.

Now our elders want us to sow
and to reap, to save what we've earned.
Just wait a minute. Soon we'll be ready to go.
Just wait a minute. Soon we'll be willing to show
exactly the lessons we've learned!

Dieter P. Lotze

Chor der Fräuleins

Wir hämmern auf die Schreibmaschinen.
Das ist genau, als spielten wir Klavier.
Wer Geld besitzt, braucht keines zu verdienen.
Wir haben keins. Drum hämmern wir.

Wir winden keine Jungfernkränze mehr.
Wir überwanden sie mit viel Vergnügen.
Zwar gibt es Herrn, die stört das sehr.
Die müssen wir belügen.

Zweimal pro Woche wird die Nacht
mit Liebelei und heißem Mund,
als wär man Mann und Frau, verbracht.
Das ist so schön! Und außerdem gesund.

Es wär nicht besser, wenn es anders wäre.
Uns braucht kein innrer Missionar zu retten!
Wer murmelt düster von verlorner Ehre?
Seid nur so treu wie wir, in euren Betten!

Nur wenn wir Kinder sehn, die lustig spielen
und Bälle fangen mit Geschrei,
und weinen, wenn sie auf die Nase fielen—
dann sind wir traurig. Doch das geht vorbei.

Kennst Du das Land, wo die Kanonen blühn?

Kennst Du das Land, wo die Kanonen blühn?
Du kennst es nicht? Du wirst es kennenlernen!
Dort stehn die Prokuristen stolz und kühn
in den Büros, als wären es Kasernen.

The Typist Chorus

We pound this damned machine as if to break it.
Just like a piano, except, of course, the sound.
Those who have money do not have to make it.
We haven't any. That is why we pound.

For us no more the blush of maiden rose.
We rose above it. And enjoyed it quite, too.
Some gentlemen recoil at this. And those
we are forced to lie to.

Two nights a week, or three, we have a man's
lovemaking and hot lips to thrill us through.
And we are man and wife. That is romance.
And it is wonderful. And healthy, too.

If things were otherwise, they'd be no better.
We need no missionary's help or threats.
Have we no honor? Is that what you mutter?
Just be as faithful in your marriage beds.

But only when we watch a child that chases
another—hear them shout as they dash past,
or howling when they've fallen on their faces—
we feel sad. But it doesn't last.

John Simon

Know'st Thou the Land Where Canons Stand in Flower?

Know'st thou the land where canons stand in flower?
You do not know it? Well, you will!
Each senior clerk there likes to show his power
to run his office like some army drill.

Dort wachsen unterm Schlips Gefreitenknöpfe.
Und unsichtbare Helme trägt man dort.
Gesichter hat man dort, doch keine Köpfe.
Und wer zu Bett geht, pflanzt sich auch schon fort!

Wenn dort ein Vorgesetzter etwas will
—und es ist sein Beruf etwas zu wollen—
steht der Verstand erst stramm und zweitens still.
Die Augen rechts! Und mit dem Rückgrat rollen!

Die Kinder kommen dort mit kleinen Sporen
und mit gezognem Scheitel auf die Welt.
Dort wird man nicht als Zivilist geboren.
Dort wird befördert, wer die Schnauze hält.

Kennst Du das Land? Es könnte glücklich sein.
Es könnte glücklich sein und glücklich machen!
Dort gibt as Äcker, Kohle, Stahl und Stein
und Fleiß und Kraft und andre schöne Sachen.

Selbst Geist und Güte gibt's dort dann und wann!
Und wahres Heldentum. Doch nicht bei vielen.
Dort steckt ein Kind in jedem zweiten Mann.
Das will mit Bleisoldaten spielen.

Dort reift die Freiheit nicht. Dort bleibt sie grün.
Was man auch baut—es werden stets Kasernen.
Kennst Du das Land, wo die Kanonen blühn?
Du kennst es nicht? Du wirst es kennenlernen!

There sergeant's stripes appear in proper places
beneath grey flannel suits. Their unseen helmets sure look great.
They don't sport heads there, they have only faces.
At night they go to bed merely to procreate.

And if a boss should utter some request
—which after all is just his right divine—
one's mind jumps to attention, his behest
makes it stand still. Eyes right! And roll your spine!

All children born within this nation
arrive with parted hair, and little spurs wear they.
No man achieves through birth civilian station.
If you want to advance, always shut up, obey!

Know'st thou this land? How happy it could feel,
still happier it could become by sharing
its wealth: rich fields, and coal, and steel,
and diligence there is, and strength, and caring.

And even wisdom, goodness can be seen.
True heroism, too, is not unknown.
But children hide within most men, quite keen
to play with leaden soldiers of their own.

No freedom flourishes, it's crushed by power.
Barracks are built on every hill.
Know'st thou the land where canons stand in flower?
You do not know it? Well, you will.

Dieter P. Lotze

Der Mensch ist gut

Der Mensch ist gut! Da gibt es nichts zu lachen!
In Lesebüchern schmeckt das wie Kompott.
Der Mensch ist gut. Da kann kann man gar nichts machen.
Er hat das, wie man hört, vom lieben Gott.

Einschränkungshalber spricht man zwar von Kriegen.
Wohl weil der letzte Krieg erst neulich war . . .
Doch: ließ man denn die Krüppel draußen liegen?
Die Witwen kriegten sogar Honorar!

Der Mensch ist gut! Wenn er noch besser wäre,
wär er zu gut für die bescheidne Welt.
Auch die Moral hat ihr Gesetz der Schwere:
Der schlechte Kerl kommt hoch—der Gute fällt.

Das ist so, wie es ist, geschickt gemacht.
Gott will es so. Not lehrt bekanntlich beten.
Er hat sich das nicht übel ausgedacht
und läßt uns um des Himmels Willen treten.

Der Mensch ist gut. Und darum geht's ihm schlecht.
Denn wenn's ihm besser ginge, wär er böse.
Drum betet: »Herr Direktor, quäl uns recht!«
Gott will es so. Und sein System hat Größe.

Der Mensch ist gut. Drum haut ihm in die Fresse!
Drum seid so gut: und seid so schlecht, wie's geht!
Drückt Löhne! Zelebriert die Leipziger Messe!
Der Himmel hat für sowas immer Interesse.—
Der Mensch bleibt gut, weil ihr den Kram versteht.

Man Is Good

Man, as you know, is good. Let no one doubt it.
So say the books on every classroom shelf.
Yes, man is good. There's no two ways about it.
He has that, we are told, from God Himself.

There are, of course, those wars one sometimes mentions;
the last one happened just the other day.
But have the widows been denied their pensions?
Or were the dead left rotting where they lay?

Sure, man is good. If he were any better,
he might just find our modest world too small.
Morality has a direction setter
which makes the bad guys rise, the good ones fall.

This all makes sense. It is a clever scheme.
One gets religion if one has to suffer.
You gather from this oft-repeated theme
that it is God Who makes existence tougher.

And thus, while man is good, his luck is bad,
for were it otherwise, he would be vicious.
So let us pray: boss, kindly drive us mad!
God wills it, and His system is judicious.

Since man is good, kick him in his posterior!
Make it, for goodness' sake, a hefty kick!
Cut wages! Celebrate a mass hysteria!
Let Heaven smile while life for us grows drearier!
Man will stay good because you know the trick.

Karl F. Ross

Wieso warum?

Warum sind tausend Kilo eine Tonne?
Warum ist dreimal Drei nicht Sieben?
Warum dreht sich die Erde um die Sonne?
Warum heißt Erna Erna statt Yvonne?
Und warum hat das Luder nicht geschrieben?

Warum ist Professoren alles klar?
Warum ist schwarzer Schlips zum Frack verboten?
Warum erfährt man nie, wie alles war?
Warum bleibt Gott grundsätzlich unsichtbar?
Und warum reißen alte Herren Zoten?

Warum darf man sein Geld nicht selber machen?
Warum bringt man sich nicht zuweilen um?
Warum trägt man im Winter Wintersachen?
Warum darf man, wenn jemand stirbt, nicht lachen?
Und warum fragt der Mensch bei jedem Quark: Warum?

Sachliche Romanze

Als sie einander acht Jahre kannten
(und man darf sagen: sie kannten sich gut),
kam ihre Liebe plötzlich abhanden.
Wie andern Leuten ein Stock oder Hut.

Sie waren traurig, betrugen sich heiter,
versuchten Küsse, als ob nichts sei,
und sahen sich an und wußten nicht weiter.
Da weinte sie schließlich. Und er stand dabei.

Why, For What Reason?

Why do a thousand kilos make a ton?
Why cannot three times three make seven?
Why does the planet earth spin round the sun?
Why call Mabel Mabel, not Yvonne?
And why has the silly bitch not written?

Why are professors thought to be so wise?
Why is a black tie incorrect with tails?
Why is the past obscure to our eyes?
Why is God hidden from us in the skies?
And why do obscene jokes old men regale?

Why are we not allowed to print our money?
Why not for suicide express a yearn?
Why in the cold of winter wear warm wool?
Why not, when someone dies, laugh like a fool?
And why ask why at every twist and turn?

E. L. Kanes

Matter-of-Fact Romance

When they had known each other for eight years
(and one might freely say, known through and through),
their love got lost. As in some house a shoe
or walking stick suddenly disappears.

Sad, they deceived each other gaily. Kept
embracing as if all were as before.
Looked at each other then. And could no more.
At last she cried. And he stood there, inept.

Vom Fenster aus konnte man Schiffen winken.
Er sagte, es wäre schon Viertel nach Vier
und Zeit, irgendwo Kaffee zu trinken.
Nebenan übte ein Mensch Klavier.

Sie gingen ins kleinste Café am Ort
und rührten in ihren Tassen.
Am Abend sasen sie immer noch dort.
Sie saßen allein, und sie sprachen kein Wort
und konnten es einfach nicht fassen.

Fantasie von übermorgen

Und als der nächste Krieg begann,
da sagten die Frauen: Nein!
und schlossen Bruder, Sohn und Mann
fest in der Wohnung ein.

Dann zogen sie, in jedem Land,
wohl vor des Hauptmanns Haus
und hielten Stöcke in der Hand
und holten die Kerls heraus.

Sie legten jeden übers Knie,
der diesen Krieg befahl:
die Herren der Bank und Industrie,
den Minister und General.

Da brach so mancher Stock entzwei.
Und manches Großmaul schwieg.
In allen Ländern gab's Geschrei,
und nirgends gab es Krieg.

From the window you could wave to ships. Then at once
he said it was already half past four,
and time to go somewhere for coffee and buns.
Someone was practicing his scales next door.

They picked a café of which no one had heard,
and stirred their cups without respite.
When evening came, they still sat there and stirred.
They sat alone, and did not say a word,
and simply could not grasp it.

John Simon

Futuristic Fantasy

And when another war came on,
the women shouted: No!
And locked up brother, mate and son
and did not let them go.

They then marched out in every land,
with cudgels long and stout,
down to the local high command
and dragged the captains out.

They gave a dose of healthy spanks
to all who'd called for war:
to heads of industry and banks,
to general and governor.

A lot of clubs were split in two
and many a loudmouth stilled.
In every land was much ado
and yet no blood was spilled.

Die Frauen gingen dann wieder nach Haus,
zum Bruder und Sohn und Mann,
und sagten ihnen, der Krieg sei aus!
Die Männer starrten zum Fenster hinaus
und sahn die Frauen nicht an . . .

Ragout Fin de Siècle

(Im Hinblick auf gewisse Lokale)

Hier können kaum die Kenner
in Herz und Nieren schauen.
Hier sind die Frauen Männer.
Hier sind die Männer Frauen.

Hier tanzen die Jünglinge selbstbewußt
im Abendkleid und mit Gummibrust
und sprechen höchsten Diskant.
Hier haben die Frauen Smokings an
und reden tief wie der Weihnachtsmann
und stecken Zigarren in Brand.

Hier stehen die Männer vorm Spiegel stramm
und schminken sich selig die Haut.
Hier hat man als Frau keinen Bräutigam.
Hier hat jede Frau eine Braut.

Hier wurden vor lauter Perversion
Vereinzelte wieder normal.
Und käme Dante in eigner Person—
er fräße vor Schreck Veronal.

Hier findet sich kein Schwein zurecht.
Die Echten sind falsch, die Falschen echt,
und alles mischt sich im Topf,
und Schmerz macht Spaß, und Lust zeugt Zorn,
und Oben ist unten, und Hinten ist vorn.
Man greift sich an den Kopf.

The women then, their battle won
and calling it a day,
went home to brother, mate and son
and told them that the war was done. . . .
The men just looked away.

Karl F. Ross

Latter-Day Stew

Here even the connoisseurs'
insight is rather dim.
Here all the hims are hers.
And every her a him.

Here youths are dancing, self-possessed,
in low-cut gown and rubber breast,
and talk in treble or higher.
Here a tux is what a woman wears—
with voice as deep as a grizzly bear's
and black cigar afire.

Here gentlemen crowd the powder-room
and blissfully paint their hides.
Here as a woman one has no groom.
Here all the women have brides.

Here, out of sheer perversion, quite
a few went normal. Lord knows,
were Dante among us now, in his fright
he'd gulp down an overdose.

Here a pig wouldn't know what role to take.
The fakes are real, the real ones fake,
and all mingle in one bed.
Here pain makes merry, pleasure sore,
and up is down, behind before.
One has to hold one's head.

Von mir aus, schlaft euch selber bei!
Und schlaft mit Drossel, Fink und Star
und Brehms gesamter Vögelschar!
Mir ist es einerlei.

Nur, schreit nicht dauernd wie am Spieß,
was ihr für tolle Kerle wärt!
Bloß weil ihr hintenrum verkehrt,
seid ihr noch nicht Genies.

Na ja, das wäre dies.

Kurzgefaßter Lebenslauf

Wer nicht zur Welt kommt, hat nicht viel verloren.
Er sitzt im All auf einem Baum und lacht.
Ich wurde seinerzeit als Kind geboren,
eh ich's gedacht.

Die Schule, wo ich viel vergessen habe,
bestritt seitdem den größten Teil der Zeit.
Ich war ein patentierter Musterknabe.
Wie kam das bloß? Es tut mir jetzt noch leid.

Dann gab es Weltkrieg, statt der großen Ferien.
Ich trieb es mit der Fußartillerie.
Dem Globus lief das Blut aus den Arterien.
Ich lebte weiter. Fragen Sie nicht, wie.

Bis dann die Inflation und Leipzig kamen;
mit Kant und Gotisch, Börse und Büro,
mit Kunst und Politik und jungen Damen.
Und sonntags regnete es sowieso.

Go copulate with yourselves, go on,
if you please, with starling, finch, or rook—
with every bird in Audubon!
For all I care, have the book.

I just wish that each of you wouldn't roar
like hell what a hell of a guy he is.
Just because you traffic by the back door,
you're not yet geniuses.

So much for that, I guess.

John Simon

A Few Personal Particulars

The man who's never born need not get wild.
He just sits some place else and laughs at life.
For my part, I was born a little child,
Before I could say 'knife'.

The school that made me such an empty head
Has been in my thoughts almost ever since.
I was a model pupil (patented).
Today remembering it still makes me wince.

Instead of holidays we had World War.
They put me into the Artillery.
The world was dripping blood from every artery.
I went on living. Don't ask what for.

Inflation came and I had much to do:
With Kant and Gothic, stock exchange and office,
With art and politics and girlfriends too.
And Sundays it would rain on top of this.

Nun bin ich zirka 31 Jahre
und habe eine kleine Versfabrik.
Ach, an den Schläfen blühn schon graue Haare,
und meine Freunde werden langsam dick.

Ich setze mich sehr gerne zwischen Stühle.
Ich säge an dem Ast, auf dem wir sitzen.
Ich gehe durch die Gärten der Gefühle,
die tot sind, und bepflanze sie mit Witzen.

Auch ich muß meinen Rucksack selber tragen!
Der Rucksack wächst. Der Rücken wird nicht breiter.
Zusammenfassend läßt sich etwa sagen:
Ich kam zur Welt und lebe trotzdem weiter.

Primaner in Uniform

Der Rektor trat, zum Abendbrot,
bekümmert in den Saal.
Der Klassenbruder Kern sei tot.
Das war das erste Mal.

Wir saßen bis zur Nacht im Park
und dachten lange nach.
Kurt Kern, gefallen bei Langemarck,
saß zwischen uns und sprach.

Dann lasen wir wieder Daudet und Vergil
und wurden zu Ostern versetzt.
Dann sagte man uns, dass Heimbold fiel.
Und Rochlitz sei schwer verletzt.

Der Rektor Jobst war Theolog
für Gott und Vaterland.
Und jedem, der in den Weltkrieg zog,
gab er zuvor die Hand.

Now I am 31 or so they say,
With a small poetry business of my own.
Alas, my hair is starting to go grey,
And all my friends are getting overblown.

I like to be caught sitting on the fence,
Cut down the branch on which I choose to sit.
I walk through gardens filled with sentiments
Long dead, and scatter there a little wit.

Like others, I am my own carryall.
It's getting heavy. I can't carry more.
So let's just say to summarize it all:
That I was born, and still come back for more!

Patrick Bridgwater

Undergraduates in Uniform

One night, the dean with solemn tread
came over to our hall.
The classmate Kern had died, he said.
He was the first to fall.

That night, we gathered in the park
where silently we walked.
Kurt Kern, just killed at Langemarck,
rejoined our group and talked.

Again, we studied the poets of old
and were promoted one grade.
Then Heimbold perished, so we were told,
and Rochlitz had stopped a grenade.

The dean, Herr Jobst, was a man of the Book
for God and the Fatherland;
and none he let go, whom the army took,
without first shaking his hand.

Kerns Mutter machte ihm Besuch.
Sie ging vor Kummer krumm.
Und weinte in ihr Taschentuch
vorm Lehrerkollegium.

Der Rochlitz starb im Lazarett.
Und wir begruben ihn dann.
Im Klassenzimmer hing ein Brett,
mit den Namen der Toten daran.

Wir saßen oft im Park am Zaun.
Nie wurde mehr gespaßt.
Inzwischen fiel der kleine Braun.
Und Koßmann wurde vergast.

Der Rektor dankte Gott pro Sieg.
Die Lehrer trieben Latein.
Wir hatten Angst vor diesem Krieg.
Und dann zog man uns ein.

Wir hatten Angst. Und hofften gar,
es spräche einer Halt!
Wir waren damals achtzehn Jahr,
und das ist nicht sehr alt.

Wir dachten an Rochlitz, Braun und Kern.
Der Rektor wünschte uns Glück.
Und blieb mit Gott und den anderen Herrn
gefaßt in der Heimat zurück.

Misanthropologie

Schöne Dinge gibt es dutzendfach.
Aber keines ist so schön wie diese:
eine ausgesprochen grüne Wiese
und paar Meter veilchenblauer Bach.

Kern's mother paid on him a call;
her back was bent with grief,
and she wept in front of the teachers all
into her handkerchief.

We buried Rochlitz, when he died
upon his hospital bed,
and listed his name in class beside
the names of the other dead.

We often to the park went down
to gather on the grass.
Then came the death of little Braun
and Kossmann was felled by gas.

For every victory report
the dean would praise God's name.
We were afraid of this deadly sport,
and then our draft call came.

We were afraid, and hoped—perhaps—
that someone stop this strife;
we were then eighteen-year-old chaps
and hadn't seen much of life.

The dean wished us a fond adieu
(we thought of Rochlitz and Braun)
as he, with God and the rest of his crew,
stayed bravely behind in the town.

Karl F. Ross

Misanthropology

Beauty is to be found in every nook.
But none more lovely than this country scene:
a meadow of a perfect shade of green
and a stretch of violet-colored brook.

Und man kneift sich. Doch das ist kein Traum.
Mit der edlen Absicht, sich zu läutern,
kniet man zwischen Blumen, Gras und Kräutern.
Und der Bach schlägt einen Purzelbaum.

Also das, denkt man, ist die Natur!
Man beschließt, in Anbetracht des Schönen,
mit der Welt sich endlich zu versöhnen.
Und ist froh, daß man ins Grüne fuhr.

Doch man bleibt nicht lange so naiv.
Plötzlich tauchen Menschen auf und schreien.
Und schon wieder ist die Welt zum Speien.
Und das Gras legt sich vor Abscheu schief.

Eben war die Landschaft noch so stumm.
Und der Wiesenteppich war so samten.
Und schon trampeln diese gottverdammten
Menschen wie in Sauerkraut herum.

Und man kommt, geschult durch das Erlebnis,
wieder mal zu folgendem Ergebnis:
Diese Menschheit ist nichts weiter als
eine Hautkrankheit des Erdenballs.

Anmerkung: Man sollte die meisten Menschen mit einer
Substanz bestreichen dürfen, die unsichtbar macht.

Dem Revolutionär Jesus zum Geburtstag

Zweitausend Jahre sind es fast,
seit du die Welt verlassen hast,
du Opferlamm des Lebens!
Du gabst den Armen ihren Gott.
Du littest durch der Reichen Spott.
Du tatest es vergebens!

And it's no dream. A pinch tends to confirm.
To cleanse the soul one gives in to an urge
to kneel among the flowers, grass and herbs.
Head over heels the brook, too, seems to turn.

So this is nature, one has to conclude.
In beauty's contemplation one decides
with one and all to become reconciled.
Quite grateful for this country interlude.

But it's not long before naïveté fades.
Out of the blue people appear and howl.
And once again the world becomes quite foul.
And in disgust the grass averts its blades.

Until just now the landscape lay quite still.
The meadow carpet had a velvet sheen.
And now the goddamned people can be seen
trampling down all the loveliness at will.

And being faced with such confusion,
one must perforce reach this conclusion:
man's role on earth is pure and simple
but that of an obnoxious pimple.

Note: One ought to be able to coat most people with a substance which would make them invisible.

E. L. Kanes

To Jesus, Revolutionary, on His Birthday

Two-thousand years went almost by
since you did suffer, preach and die
with no success whatever.
You led the poor man to his Lord;
you scorned the rich man and his hoard—
you failed in your endeavor.

Du sahst Gewalt und Polizei.
Du wolltest alle Menschen frei
und Frieden auf der Erde.
Du wußtest, wie das Elend tut
und wolltest alle Menschen gut,
damit es schöner werde!

Du warst ein Revolutionär
und machtest dir das Leben schwer
mit Schiebern und Gelehrten.
Du hast die Freiheit stets beschützt
und doch den Menschen nichts genützt.
Du kamst an die Verkehrten!

Du kämpftest tapfer gegen sie
und gegen Staat und Industrie
und die gesamte Meute.
Bis man an dir, weil nichts verfing,
Justizmord, kurzerhand, beging.
Es war genau wie heute.

Die Menschen wurden nicht gescheit.
Am wenigsten die Christenheit,
trotz allem Händefalten.
Du hattest sie vergeblich lieb.
Du starbst umsonst. Und alles blieb
beim alten.

Und wo bleibt das Positive, Herr Kästner?

Und immer wieder schickt ihr mir Briefe,
in denen ihr, dick unterstrichen, schreibt:
»Herr Kästner, wo bleibt das Positive?«
Ja, weiß der Teufel, wo das bleibt.

You knew the pangs of poverty
and wanted everybody free
from want, and fear, and fetter.
You tried to help as best you could
and wanted everybody good
so that this world be better.

You were rebelliously inclined
and bared your sorrow-laden mind
to men of clout and learning.
You challenged power and police
and strove for liberty and peace—
none understood your yearning.

You fought the captains and the kings
and all their rotten underlings
with bravery and passion.
Till, when your zeal did not subside,
they had you tried and crucified.
(That trick is still in fashion.)

Mankind did not find sanity—
especially Christianity,
inspite of pious mumbling.
You loved them all, to no avail;
you died in vain, and left them frail
and fumbling.

Karl F. Ross

How About Something Positive, Mr. Kästner?

Lots of your letters contain this suggestion:
"Hey! What about the positive side?"
Yes, what about it? A very good question.
I've never found it, as hard as I tried.

Noch immer räumt ihr dem Guten und Schönen
den leeren Platz überm Sofa ein.
Ihr wollt euch noch immer nicht dran gewöhnen,
gescheit und trotzdem tapfer zu sein.

Ihr braucht schon wieder mal Vaseline,
mit der ihr das trockene Brot beschmiert.
Ihr sagt schon wieder, mit gläubiger Miene:
»Der siebente Himmel wird frisch tapeziert!«

Ihr streut euch Zucker über die Schmerzen
und denkt, unter Zucker verschwänden sie.
Ihr baut schon wieder Balkons vor die Herzen
und nehmt die strampelnde Seele aufs Knie.

Die Spezies Mensch ging aus dem Leime
und mit ihr Haus und Staat und Welt.
Ihr wünscht, daß ich's hübsch zusammenreime,
und denkt, daß es dann zusammenhält?

Ich will nicht schwindeln. Ich werde nicht schwindeln.
Die Zeit ist schwarz, ich mach euch nichts weis.
Es gibt genug Lieferanten von Windeln.
Und manche liefern zum Selbstkostenpreis.

Habt Sonne in sämtlichen Körperteilen
und wickelt die Sorgen in Seidenpapier!
Doch tut es rasch. Ihr müßt euch beeilen.
Sonst werden die Sorgen größer als ihr.

Die Zeit liegt im Sterben. Bald wird sie begraben.
Im Osten zimmern sie schon den Sarg.
Ihr möchtet gern euren Spaß dran haben . . . ?
Ein Friedhof ist kein Lunapark.

You're saving a place of honor forever
above your couch for the good and sublime:
why is it, then, that you cannot be clever
and also courageous at the same time?

You keep on looking for calamine lotion
to spread on the stale old bread that you chew.
You still assert, with trusting devotion:
"They're painting the Seventh Heaven like new!"

You coat your sores with sugar, as always,
believing that sugar will make them whole.
You shield your hearts with sheltering hallways
and rock to sleep the unruly soul.

The species Man is under the weather
and so are world and home and state.
You wish that I rhyme it nicely together
and think that it won't disintegrate?

I won't mislead you about the issues;
I cannot make light of the dark times we face.
Go, get yourselves a supply of tissues,
you even may find them on sale in some place.

Just roll your troubles in beautiful wrapping,
keep sunny side up from shoulder to shoe!
But hurry up and don't be caught napping
or else those troubles will rise above you.

This era of ours is doomed and is dying.
Its coffin is being built in the East.
You want to have fun when you ought to be crying?
A graveyard is no site for a feast.

Karl F. Ross

Das letzte Kapitel

Am 12. Juli des Jahres 2003
lief folgender Funkspruch rund um die Erde:
daß ein Bombengeschwader der Luftpolizei
die gesamte Menschheit ausrotten werde.

Die Weltregierung, so wurde erklärt, stelle fest,
daß der Plan, endgültig Frieden zu stiften,
sich gar nicht anders verwirklichen läßt,
als alle Beteiligten zu vergiften.

Zu fliehen, wurde erklärt, habe keinen Zweck.
Nicht eine Seele dürfe am Leben bleiben.
Das neue Giftgas krieche in jedes Versteck.
Man habe nicht einmal nötig, sich selbst zu entleiben.

Am 13. Juli flogen von Boston eintausend
mit Gas und Bazillen belandene Flugzeuge fort
und vollbrachten, rund um den Globus sausend,
den von der Weltregierung befohlenen Mord.

Die Menschen krochen winselnd unter die Betten.
Sie stürzten in ihre Keller und in den Wald.
Das Gift hing gelb wie Wolken über den Städten.
Millionen Leichen lagen auf dem Asphalt.

Jeder dachte, er könne dem Tod entgehen.
Keiner entging dem Tod, und die Welt wurde leer.
Das Gift war überall. Es schlich wie auf Zehen.
Es lief die Wüsten entlang. Und es schwamm übers Meer.

Die Menschen lagen gebündelt wie faulende Garben.
Andre hingen wie Puppen zum Fenster heraus.
Die Tiere im Zoo schrien schrecklich, bevor sie starben.
Und langsam löschten die großen Hochöfen aus.

The Ultimate Chapter

On the twelfth of July in two thousand and three,
By radio this message was quickly related:
A squadron of air police bombers will see
That mankind at last is exterminated.

World government sources said, so it was learned,
That the plan for a lasting and general peace
Entailed the destruction of all concerned.
How else, it was argued, would wars ever cease?

It was further explained that escape would be vain,
For general extinction had been declared.
Suicides were relieved of their trouble and pain.
From the poisonous gas none could be spared.

On the thirteenth the planes from Boston departed
With poisonous gas to accomplish their deed.
They circled the globe and quickly imparted
The death the elected officials decreed.

People crawled whimpering under their beds.
They scrambled to cellars and to their defeat,
While the poison worked as a summer cloud spreads.
Millions of corpses lay about on the street.

Everyone thought he might weather this blight.
Everyone died. And the world became bare.
The poison came like a thief in the night.
It swept along deserts, it rode on the air.

Corpses were whirled along by this tide.
From the windows like puppets dangled the dead.
The zoos sent up screams as the animals died,
And the furnaces cooled which no one had fed.

Dampfer schwankten im Meer, beladen mit Toten.
Und weder Weinen noch Lachen war mehr auf der Welt.
Die Flugzeuge irrten, mit tausend toten Piloten,
unter dem Himmel und sanken brennend ins Feld.

Jetzt hatte die Menschheit endlich erreicht, was sie wollte.
Zwar war die Methode nicht ausgesprochen human.
Die Erde war aber endlich still und zufrieden und rollte,
völlig beruhigt, ihre bekannte elliptische Bahn.

Die Entwicklung der Menschheit

Einst haben die Kerls auf den Bäumen gehockt,
behaart und mit böser Visage.
Dann hat man sie aus dem Urwald gelockt
und die Welt asphaltiert und aufgestockt,
bis zur dreißigsten Etage.

Da saßen sie nun, den Flöhen entflohn,
in zentralgeheizten Räumen.
Da sitzen sie nun am Telefon.
Und es herrscht noch genau derselbe Ton
wie seinerzeit auf den Bäumen.

Sie hören weit. Sie sehen fern.
Sie sind mit dem Weltall in Fühlung.
Sie putzen die Zähne. Sie atmen modern.
Die Erde ist ein gebildeter Stern
mit sehr viel Wasserspülung.

Sie schießen die Briefschaften durch ein Rohr.
Sie jagen und züchten Mikroben.
Sie versehn die Natur mit allem Komfort.
Sie fliegen steil in den Himmel empor
und bleiben zwei Wochen oben.

Liners turned into graveyards on water.
Tears and laughter no longer abounded,
The originators of all this slaughter,
After losing their pilots, were finally grounded.

Mankind had harvested what it intended.
The method was hardly devoid of some force.
Earth however was fairly contented,
And resumed its well-known elliptical course.

Richard and Mary Anne Exner

The Ascent of Man

Once they lived high up in the trees,
mean faced, all covered with hair.
Then they were lured from the jungle with ease,
and the world was blacktopped for fellows like these,
and thirty-floor buildings rose up in the air.

There they now dwelt in the temperate zone,
in heated apartments, escaped from the fleas.
There they now sit by their telephone,
and yet they're still using the very same tone
as they did when they lived in the trees.

Voices and pictures can reach them from far;
To distant planets their signals keep rushing.
They brush their teeth: quite health-conscious they are.
Earth is a thoroughly civilized star
Where plenty of water is flushing.

Through tubes their pneumatic messages race.
And creature comforts they amply provide.
Microbes they've learned to breed and to chase.
Their flying contraptions soar up into space
and after two weeks come home from their ride.

Was ihre Verdauung übrigläßt,
das verarbeiten sie zu Watte.
Sie spalten Atome. Sie heilen Inzest.
Und sie stellen durch Stiluntersuchungen fest,
daß Cäsar Plattfüße hatte.

So haben sie mit dem Kopf und dem Mund
den Fortschritt der Menschheit geschaffen.
Doch davon mal abgesehen und
bei Lichte betrachtet sind sie im Grund
noch immer die alten Affen.

Der Handstand auf der Loreley

(Nach einer wahren Bagebenheit)

Die Loreley, bekannt als Fee und Felsen,
ist jener Fleck am Rhein, nicht weit von Bingen,
wo früher Schiffer mit verdrehten Hälsen,
von blonden Haaren schwärmend, untergingen.

Wir wandeln uns. Die Schiffer inbegriffen.
Der Rhein ist reguliert und eingedämmt.
Die Zeit vergeht. Man stirbt nicht mehr beim Schiffen,
bloß weil ein blondes Weib sich dauernd kämmt.

Nichtsdestotrotz geschieht auch heutzutage
noch manches, was der Steinzeit ähnlich sieht.
So alt ist keine deutsche Heldensage,
daß sie nicht doch noch Helden nach sich zieht.

Erst neulich machte auf der Loreley
hoch überm Rhein ein Turner einen Handstand!
Von allen Dampfern tönte Angstgeschrei,
als er kopfüber oben auf der Wand stand.

There is no waste: what they digest,
Is changed into cotton, and starches.
They split the atom. They cure incest,
And conclude from a careful stylistic test
That Caesar had fallen arches.

Thus with their language and power of mind
They fashioned the progress of this human race.
But take a close look and study their kind,
forget all the trappings, and this you will find:
The same old monkeys still stare in your face.

Dieter P. Lotze

The Handstand on the Lorelei

Not far from Bingen is the Lorelei,
That Rhenish maid, as monument now cherished,
Where formerly the sailors, necks awry,
Enchanted by her golden locks have perished.

All of us, including sailors, change.
The Rhine's now regulated everywhere.
Time passes. We would think it very strange
To drown because some woman combs her hair.

Yet, strange to say, today still things occur
Reminding one of prehistoric ways.
The age of German legends can't deter
Arousing heroes even nowadays.

A gynmast tried a handstand recently!
Above the Rhine atop the Lorelei.
As with his legs he greeted destiny,
From all the steamers rose an anxious cry.

Er stand, als ob er auf dem Barren stünde.
Mit hohlem Kreuz. Und lustbetonten Zügen.
Man fragte nicht: Was hatte er für Gründe?
Er war ein Held. Das dürfte wohl genügen.

Er stand, verkehrt, im Abendsonnenscheine.
Da trübte Wehmut seinen Turnerblick.
Er dachte an die Loreley von Heine.
Und stürzte ab. Und brach sich das Genick.

Er starb als Held. Man muß ihn nicht beweinen.
Sein Handstand war vom Schicksal überstrahlt.
Ein Augenblick mit zwei gehobnen Beinen
ist nicht zu teuer mit dem Tod bezahlt!

P. S. Eins wäre allerdings noch nachzutragen:
Der Turner hinterließ uns Frau und Kind.
Hinwiederum, man soll sie nicht beklagen.
Weil im Bezirk der Helden und der Sagen
die Überlebenden nicht wichtig sind.

Lessing

Das, was er schrieb, war manchmal Dichtung,
doch um zu dichten schrieb er nie.
Es gab kein Ziel. Er fand die Richtung.
Er war ein Mann und kein Genie.

Er lebte in der Zeit der Zöpfe,
und er trug selber seinen Zopf.
Doch kamen seitdem viele Köpfe
und niemals wieder so ein Kopf.

As if he stood upon the bars, he stood.
His back was arched and his expression lustful.
Don't ask for reasons, don't say what's the good.
He was a hero. Don't be so distrustful!

In the evening sun he stood with head towards China.
Then melancholy glazed this gymnast's sight.
He thought of Lorelei, the one by Heine,
And broke his neck in falling from that height.

He died a hero. Let there be no rue.
And glorious fate has made his handstand splendid.
One moment with both legs against the blue,
A life was not in vain that thus had ended.

PS. It would be nice to add a small detail:
The gymnast left for us his child and wife.
But why should we be sorry and bewail.
In realms of legend and heroic tale
He never counts who never risks his life.

Richard and Mary Anne Exner

Lessing

Sometimes the lines he penned do read like poetry,
though writing poetry was really not his plan.
There was no goal in sight. And yet a path found he.
No genius, to be sure, he truly was a man.

In those quaint times, as each man wore a queue,
He also wore a pigtail of that kind.
While later ages brought forth thinkers, too,
No one could ever match his lofty mind.

Er war ein Mann, wie keiner wieder,
obwohl er keinen Säbel schwang.
Er schlug den Feind mit Worten nieder,
und keinen gab's, den er nicht zwang.

Er stand allein und kämpfte ehrlich
und schlug der Zeit die Fenster ein.
Nichts auf der Welt macht so gefährlich,
als tapfer und allein zu sein!

He was a man. There never has been one
like him. Through merely using word and thought,
he'd fell his foes as if with sword or gun.
No enemy succeeded where he fought.

Alone he stood, and honest was his fight,
he did not mind if shattered glass would fall.
There's nothing that fills people so with fright
as one lone man who's braver than they all!

Dieter P. Lotze

Index of Titles or First Lines

GERMAN

ENGLISH

Wilhelm Busch

Christian Morgenstern

Kurt Tucholsky

Erich Kästner

ACKNOWLEDGMENTS

Every reasonable effort has been made to locate the parties who hold rights to previously published translations reprinted here. We gratefully acknowledge permission to reprint the following:

By Wilhelm Busch—*Max and Moritz, Adventures of a Bachelor, Clement Dove,* and six poems from *The Genius of Wilhelm Busch: Comedy of Frustration: An English Anthology,* edited and translated by Walter Arndt. Copyright © 1982 by The Regents of the University of California. Reprinted by permission of the University of California Press.

By Christian Morgenstern—all thirty-nine poems from *The Gallows Songs: Christian Morgenstern's Galgenlieder: A Selection,* translated, with an introduction, by Max Knight. Copyright © 1963 by Max E. Knight. Reprinted by permission of the University of California Press.

By Kurt Tucholsky—"Essay on Man," "The Social Psychology of Holes," "Angler Compleat with Piety," "Herr Wendriner Gives a Dinner Party," and all nine poems from *What If—?: Satirical Writings of Kurt Tucholsky,* translated by Harry Zohn and Karl F. Ross (Minerva Press/Funk & Wagnalls). English translation copyright © 1967 by Harry Zohn and Karl F. Ross. Reprinted by permission of Harper & Row Publishers, Inc.

"The Creed of the Bourgeois" from *The World Is a Comedy: A Tucholsky Anthology,* translated and edited by Harry Zohn (Cambridge, Mass.: Sci-Art Publishers, 1957). Reprinted by permission of Harry Zohn.

The nine poems in German are reprinted by permission of Rowohlt Verlag, which also granted permission for the translations of "Someday Somebody Should," "Herr Wendriner in Paris," and "Herr Wendriner Can't Fall Asleep"—from Kurt Tucholski, *Gesammelte Werke,* copyright © 1960 by Rowohlt Verlag GMBH, Reinbek bei Hamburg, West Germany.

By Erich Kästner—"A Few Personal Particulars," "The Ultimate Chapter," and "The Handstand on the Lorelei" from *Let's Face It: Poems by Erich Kästner,* edited by Patrick Bridgwater (London: Jonathan Cape, 1963). Reprinted by permission of Jonathan Cape.

"The Other Possibility" from *Twenty German Poets: A Bilingual Collection,* edited, translated, and introduced by Walter Kaufmann. © Copyright, 1962, by Random House, Inc. Reprinted by permission of Hazel D. Kaufman.

The German poems are from Käster's *Herz auf Taille* (1928), *Ein Mann gibt Auskunft* (1930), *Gesang zwischen den Stühlen* (1932), *Lärm im Spiegel* (1929), and *Dr. Erich Kästners Lyrische Hausapotheke,* all published by Atrium Verlag AG, Zurich, and reprinted by permission.

THE GERMAN LIBRARY
in 100 Volumes

Introduction by Gordon Birrell
Foreword by John Gardiner

Volume 32
Heinrich Heine
Poetry and Prose
Edited by Jost Hermand and Robert C. Holub
Foreword by Alfred Kazin

Volume 39
German Poetry from 1750 to 1900
Edited by Robert M. Browning
Foreword by Michael Hamburger

Volume 44
Gottfried Keller
Stories
Edited by Frank G. Ryder
Foreword by Max Frisch

Volume 45
Wilhelm Raabe
Novels
Edited by Volkmar Sander
Foreword by Joel Agee

Volume 46
Theodore Fontane
Short Novels and Other Writings
Edited by Peter Demetz
Foreword by Peter Gay

Volume 50
Wilhelm Busch and Others
German Satirical Writings
Edited by Dieter P. Lotze and Volkmar Sander
Foreword by John Simon

Volume 55
Arthur Schnitzler
Plays and Stories
Edited by Egon Schwarz
Foreword by Stanley Elkin

Volume 70
Rainer Maria Rilke
Prose and Poetry
Edited by Egon Schwarz
Foreword by Howard Nemerov

Volume 89
Friedrich Dürrenmatt
Plays and Essays
Edited by Volkmar Sander
Foreword by Martin Esslin

Volume 98
Hans Magnus Enzensberger
Critical Essays
Edited by Reinhold Grimm and Bruce Armstrong
Foreword by John Simon